IDENTITY IN COMMUNITY:
discovering who we are together in Christ

AMY WELLNER

UNION
PRESS

MINNEAPOLIS, MN

Edited by Jana Spooner
Cover design by Karen Corrigan

ISBN: 979-8-9865686-2-1

To MJ, Erika, and Bethany –
thank you

CONTENTS

Introduction

We all have an identity. It is the aspects of our personality, beliefs, and values that make us who we are. Identity is a foundational concept that contributes to our health and well-being. It gives us a sense of self and belonging.

As believers in Jesus, our primary identity is not our nationality, political party, career sector, or familial status. These things might be important to us and can greatly impact who we are and how we live. But our primary identity is in Christ: a beloved child of God, chosen and deeply loved. We are defined by God, above all other labels, counting what he says about us as most significant, steady, and secure.

Contrary to cultural claims, we don't construct our identity; we discover it. We look to God to define us because he created us, knows us, and loves us unconditionally. We can't always follow our heart to our identity because it can be deceitful and lead us astray (Jer. 17:9). We don't look to the world to define us, because it will sell us lies about what is most important and what will give us life. How will we know what is true of us and what is not? We are invited to discover what God says about us and who he created us to be. What God says is true, and he is trustworthy.

One way we can get tripped up in pursuit of our identity is to focus only on ourselves and never on our community. American culture places a high value on individualism. God has created each of us uniquely and individually, but he has also created a family of believers who come together to reflect who he is. We reflect him in one another and in the world. We can't live the Christian life in isolation. Together, we discover who we were created to be in Christ and walk with others in this God-given identity.

While we don't work to create our identity, we sometimes need to work to believe it. It can be a struggle to understand who God says we are. It's natural to think our relationship with God is dependent on our behavior. God, in his mercy, withholds the punishment we deserve for our mistakes. We can't live up to his standard of perfection, but he doesn't punish us because of it. He offers us a perfect substitute: Jesus Christ. And he gives us even more! Not only are we not punished, but we are bestowed with blessings. We are chosen, deeply loved children of God, created in his image, heirs, and on and on and on! You are his, not because you have proven yourself worthy, but because he makes you worthy. And he gives you the grace you need to believe this, by faith.

The older I get in life and the longer I walk with God, the more I realize my struggle is not with gaining enough knowledge about God, but in deciding whether I will believe what I already know. Believing the truth about who I am in Christ brings a peace I cannot find anywhere else. The truth about who I am brings joy, hope and purpose like nothing else in this world can. Some of the identity statements that follow may be familiar to you. If so, don't skip over them. Allow God to work in your heart and mind. Ask him to reveal himself to you through these statements. While you may *know* some of these important truths about our identity in Christ, consider whether you *believe* them and how believing them changes your life.

I can be tempted to think that because these identity statements are true of other believers, they are less meaningful for me. That is a lie. God is big enough to love everyone. I can experience him individually while the guy at the table next to me in the coffee shop can experience him in a different way, at the same time.

There is danger in thinking too much of self when we consider our identity; doing so can turn into self-idolatry or what some call "navel-gazing." Allowing God to define us in the context of his nature and his work in our lives helps prevent this. We look upward to God as the source of our identity. As we work to believe it, we go inward. Looking at our identity in the context of community then moves us from an inward focus to an outward focus.

All these things that are true of us in Christ are also true of other believers, and we understand who we are in Christ more fully when we are in community with other believers. If we try to live out our identity in Christ alone, we miss out. We understand more of God when we engage with others. He reflects himself to us through his people. We are formed into the image of Christ through his body—fellow believers. God is relational and desires his people to be together in community.

Wherever your identity is rooted, it will flow out of you in how you respond to others, how you talk to yourself, and how you commune with God. Identity is a motivator. Our behavior follows where we put our identity. If our worth is in a job title, we will do whatever we need to be successful at our job. If our value is in how others perceive us, we will do whatever we can to ensure others think highly of us. If our identity is in how we perform, our relationships, our financial stability, or in Christ, it will be evident to others.

God is the giver of good things (Matt. 7:11), including our identity. Ask him to help you discover who you are in Christ and to trust him with it.

I cannot say it better than Dutch priest, professor, and writer Henri J.M. Nouwen. He writes, "This is the mystery of the Christian life: to receive a new self, a new identity, which depends not on what we can achieve, but on what we are willing to receive."

1

I am included in the family of God.

Belonging is vital. We all need to feel as though we belong to a group of people who know us, love us, and accept us. Belonging grounds us and gives us a sense of safety and security, which are basic human needs. We can experience belonging in a variety of places: the workplace, friend groups, church, sports teams, or our family.

The most significant aspect of our identity in Christ is the invitation God extends to all people to become part of his family. When we acknowledge our inability to live up to God's standards and recognize that Jesus lived the perfect life we could not (and can never) live, everything changes. God becomes our Father, and we become his children. We are given a new spiritual family, with brothers and sisters in Christ to encourage, guide, admonish, and love us. And we are asked to encourage, guide, admonish, and love our brothers and sisters in Christ.

The word "family" is loaded with meaning. You may have a positive experience with family, whether biological or not. You may have a negative experience with family, full of pain and brokenness. Likely, you have a mix of both experiences. Families come in all shapes and sizes and impact us greatly as children and adults. We bring this reality into our relationship with God because our relationship with him is one of family. He is our Father, and we are his children.

You may have had experiences of belonging in faith communities, such as churches, small groups, or Bible studies. You also may have had experiences where you felt like you didn't belong; you felt unseen, disconnected, or "othered."

I grew up attending church. I don't remember a time when I didn't believe in God. But during my teenage years, I had a sense that there was more to faith than just believing in God and sitting in a church pew on Sunday morning. I wasn't sure what else there was, but I was aware that God had a standard for me to live up to in life, and I just couldn't do it. I felt like trying to be a good person wasn't enough. How good was good enough? How would I know?

In college, I met a group of people who acted differently from anyone else I'd met. They had a genuine love and interest in others. They welcomed anyone into their group, no matter their beliefs. I began to see God's care for me lived out through these friendships. They celebrated with me over good news and supported me through hard things. They had a joy and a lightness I had not seen in others.

I felt a deep sense of belonging with this group. It was a safe place to question my beliefs about God and admit my doubts. I didn't always understand everything or agree with everything we discussed. But I was genuinely cared for, encouraged, and welcomed. Throughout my life, I've felt varying levels of belonging with Christian groups and churches. There's no perfect group; in each one I have joined, there have been times when I felt like I didn't belong. But even with those feelings, whether they were true or not, I experienced more belonging in those groups than in most others outside of my faith.

The familial nature of our identity is perhaps the easiest category in which to see how our identity in Christ is communal. It naturally involves others. There's no "being a Christian" on your own. Being a part of the family of God means we belong. And belonging is all about seeing those around us, and being with them and for them. We belong to God, but we also belong to one another.

This completely changes how we live our lives. God establishes a new kingdom of his people, one that is not bound by race, ethnicity, gender, social class, age, or even time itself. In this kingdom, we have a responsibility to one another and for one another. When someone in my community is hurting, I hurt. When someone in my community is celebrating, I celebrate. This can be hard for those of us who grew up in a culture that places a high value on individualism and self-sufficiency. I encourage you to press in and consider how belonging to God and to others impacts you.

In this section, we focus on being a part of God's family: We are children of God, we are part of the body of Christ, we are united with Christ, we are made in the image of God, and we are chosen.

I am a child of God.

See how very much our Father loves us, for he calls us his children, and that is what we are! But the people who belong to this world don't recognize that we are God's children because they don't know him. Dear friends, we are already God's children, but he has not yet shown us what we will be like when Christ appears. But we do know that we will be like him, for we will see him as he really is.

—1 John 3:1–2 NLT

Throughout Scripture, we read about our identity as children of God. This is a secure status that is unchanging and not dependent on anything we ourselves can do. The individual identity as a child of God is astounding: He is our Father who desires intimate fellowship with us. He has a loving tenderness and compassion toward us (Ps. 103:13). We are children by faith (Gal. 3:26). He provides and cares for us (Matt. 6:26).

As if that wasn't enough, the communal aspect of being a child of God is even more incredible: We are all part of God's family. We are adopted by God through faith in the saving work of Jesus (Eph. 1:5). Adoption is a legal change in status, an action in which someone chooses to participate. On adoption day, a judge declares a child permanently accepted into a new family.

The child is there at his parents' request, chosen by them before he could do anything good at all. The child becomes legally part of their family forever.

Because of this spiritual adoption, I have brothers and sisters in Christ who love and care for me (Rom. 12:10). God sets the lonely in families (Ps. 68:6), and we suffer together and rejoice together (1 Cor. 12:26). Through Jesus Christ, God chooses to adopt us into his family, and us being a part of his family brings him joy! Scripture says:

> [Jesus] came into the very world he created, but the world didn't recognize him. He came to his own people, and even they rejected him. But to all who believed him and accepted him, he gave the right to become children of God. They are reborn—not with a physical birth resulting from human passion or plan, but a birth that comes from God. (John 1:10–13 NLT)

This status as members of his family will never change and is secure for the rest of our lives. We never have to question whether God wants us.

In a sermon from the nineties, pastor and author Tim Keller described how we can incorrectly relate to God through a tenant/landlord relationship.[1] In this framework, God is the landlord, and we are the tenant. We live in his house, and when we pay our rent on time, he needs to hold up his end of the deal by keeping the house in working order. He will put a roof over our heads, but we need to work for it. At any moment, the relationship could change, and we're out on the street.

Living that way is anxiety-inducing. We never know if what we've done is good enough. But our relationship with God is not a transactional one, like this tenant/landlord situation. It's a familial relationship. In this framework, God isn't our landlord, but a Father who loves unconditionally. We don't have to earn our way into his good graces. In fact, we can't. We live in his house as his child, not as his tenant. A tenant has to keep the rules. That's part of the deal. If they don't, they are kicked out of the house. A child is loved and accepted simply because they are part of the family. They can try their best to keep the rules out of respect and love, but even when they falter, their standing as part of the family does not change.

God offers us a place in his family. With that blessing, we are secure in our relationship with him, not because of anything we have done, but because Jesus reconciles us to God (Rom. 5:10). Despite our failures, our mistakes, and our inability to live like Jesus did, if we believe by faith in his sacrifice for us on the cross, we are a part of God's family (John 1:12). And that never changes. We are members of God's household forever (Eph. 2:19).

There can be times of doubt or disillusionment. We can be hurt by our fellow brothers and sisters in Christ. At times, it might feel like we're not part of the family, but this is where faith comes in (Gal. 3:26). Being children of God, together, means we are for one another, support one another, and do good to one another. We are to treat one another with dignity and respect because we are all part of the same family. This doesn't mean we never disagree, but we do so with grace and humility. We work toward unity in the midst of disagreement and seek to believe the best in one another.

***

"The enemy's greatest threat is children of God knowing who they are."
—Hosanna Wong, *You Are More Than You've Been Told*[2]

I am part of the body of Christ.

For just as the body is one and has many members, and all the members of the body, though many, are one body, so it is with Christ. For in one Spirit we were all baptized into one body—Jews or Greeks, slaves or free—and all were made to drink of one Spirit. For the body does not consist of one member but of many. . . . But as it is, God arranged the members in the body, each one of them, as he chose. If all were a single member, where would the body be? As it is, there are many parts, yet one body.

—1 Corinthians 12:12–14, 18–20 ESV

Just as God exists in relationship with himself (Father, Son, and Holy Spirit), we are made to exist in relationships with others. No matter our ethnicity, background, political affiliation, education level, occupation, or age, we all have a place in the larger body of Christ. It is within this diversity that we see the beauty and unity of Christian community.

The depth of friendship possible with another believer in Christ, despite our real or perceived differences, cannot compare with any other relationship. This friendship involves showing the heart of Christ to another person—being there with them in all their struggles and successes, praying for them, encouraging them, speaking truth when it's hard to do so, and when it might impact the friendship itself. There's nothing like it.

But community is messy. People are broken and selfish, and we contribute to the mess! For some of us, it seems easier to go it alone in life. We think that needing others shows weakness. We don't want to be seen as vulnerable. We think that depending on others is too hard and that they will let us down if we open up. We think if we do express our need for others, we will owe them something, or we will give up our power.

Needing others is a normal, human reality. In community, we experience life the way God meant it to be lived, outlined in 1 Corinthians 12:

~   God desires there to be no division in the body (v. 24).
~   If one suffers, we all suffer (v. 25).
~   If one succeeds, we all rejoice (v. 26).
~   We are individuals in Christ, and yet we are all together one body in Christ and of Christ (v. 27).

The unity of believers is a great witness to the world. In John 17, Jesus prays a prayer of unity for his disciples and for all of us:

> I pray that they will all be one, just as you and I are one—as you are in me, Father, and I am in you. And may they be in us so that the world

will believe you sent me. I have given them the glory you gave me, so they may be one as we are one. I am in them and you are in me. May they experience such perfect unity that the world will know that you sent me and that you love them as much as you love me. Father, I want these whom you have given me to be with me where I am. Then they can see all the glory you gave me because you loved me even before the world began! (John 17:21–24 NLT)

We have different purposes, callings, and crosses to bear. This is why each of us is a vital part of the body of Christ; our uniqueness matters. Some of us are hands and feet in the body of Christ, while others are eyes and ears. Each part makes up the whole. Each part is vital for a thriving community that honors God, brings him glory, and reaches out to share the love and hope of Christ with those around us.

As you read more about what it means to put our identity in Christ, individually and collectively, the truth that you are part of the body of Christ will come up again and again. It's foundational to who we are in Christ. If we want to live lives that are integrated with the rest of God's community and experience the fullness of what God has for us, we cannot escape it.

***

"Community has little to do with mutual compatibility. Similarities in educational background, psychological makeup, or social status can bring us together, but they can never be the basis for community. Community is grounded in God, who calls us together, and not in the attractiveness of people to each other. . . . The mystery of community is precisely that it embraces *all* people, whatever their individual differences may be, and allows them to live together as brothers and sisters of Christ and sons and daughters of his heavenly Father."

—Henri J.M. Nouwen, *Making All Things New*[3]

I am united with Christ.

For if we have been united with him in a death like his, we will certainly also be united with him in a resurrection like his. For we know that our old self was crucified with him so that the body ruled by sin might be done away with, that we should no longer be slaves to sin—because anyone who has died has been set free from sin. Now if we died with Christ, we believe that we will also live with him. For we know that since Christ was raised from the dead, he cannot die again; death no longer has mastery over him. The death he died, he died to sin once for all; but the life he lives, he lives to God.

—Romans 6:5–10

It is because of Jesus that we are made right with God. While we are born separated from God, Jesus restores that connection to God. Jesus, being fully God and fully man, lived a perfect, sinless life. He died a sinner's death on the cross to pay the penalty for our sins. He was resurrected, raised to new life, and is alive now, seated at the right hand of God.

Through Jesus, we are united with God, both in his death and resurrection. What does this mean? Our sinful nature and our selfish inclinations no longer have power over us. They are nailed to the cross that Christ died upon. Through Christ, we are immune from both the penalty and the power of sin. We live in union with him (Col. 2:10), are abiding in him (John 15), and are hidden in him (Col. 3:3).

As we experience this union, we grow further away from the person we were before Christ and grow more into his image and likeness (2 Cor. 3:18). Christianity is not about behavior management. We don't just try harder to be better people. When we experience union with Christ, our lives change from the inside out. The things that used to give us satisfaction don't seem to be as important anymore. We seek the things of God. We have the desires of his heart. We want what he wants.

What does it mean to be united with Christ in his resurrection? He was raised from the dead, and we will one day rise as well. We will leave behind our brokenness, internally and externally, and experience all that heaven has to offer. We get glimpses of it now, but someday, we will experience it in full. Being united with Christ in our resurrection would be enough, as he is the giver and sustainer of life and satisfies our every need. But we also get to be reunited with believers who have passed on before us. We are united in Christ together on earth, and we are united in Christ together in heaven.

We are united with Christ, just as other believers are united with Christ. Therefore, we are united with these other believers. Believers all over the world have common ground with each other in the life, death, and resurrection of Jesus. There are so many differences that can divide us, but this commonality means that we can be united across theological and cultural lines. Being united with others in Christ doesn't mean we all need to look the same, act the same, talk the same, or even believe all the exact same specific things.

For most of my life, I did not experience this union with God. I thought it was something I needed to work for, something I needed to achieve, instead of something I just needed to receive. I thought if I didn't work hard enough, God would stop loving me or forgiving me. I felt like I was living in a labor union for God, instead of a loving union with God. It took years for me to see this, after I went through a season of burnout and then depression. Those were hard years, thinking that the most important part of me was my decision to make the fulfillment of the Great Commission (Matt. 28:18–20) the only thing that mattered in my life. I was chained to this command and terrified to rest because I didn't want to let anyone down, especially not God.

But coming through the other side, I realize now that I had a warped view of what I thought the Christian life was. I saw a task list when God wanted a relationship. Instead of doing things *for* him, I could do things *with* him. He longs to experience life with his people, and if we are honest, our deepest desires and longings can be fulfilled in a loving union with him. We are made for union with God.

In his book *The Furious Longing of God*, Brennan Manning speaks of a God who "wants more than a close relationship with you and me; He seeks nothing less than union."[4] God doesn't just want some of our time, attention, and love. God wants all of us. He is patient with us as we learn and understand what that surrender looks like. The more we yield to him, the closer our union grows, and the greater our experience of him in our everyday lives. And we get to experience this union right alongside our brothers and sisters in Christ. There is enough of Jesus to go around so that everyone is offered a unique, thriving, connected union with Christ.

***

"The deepest desire of our hearts is for union with God. God created us for union with himself: This is the original purpose of our lives."

—Brennan Manning, *The Furious Longing of God*[5]

I am made in the image of God.

Then God said, "Let us make human beings in our image, to be like us. They will reign over the fish in the sea, the birds in the sky, the livestock, all the wild animals on the earth, and the small animals that scurry along the ground." So God created human beings in his own image. In the image of God he created them; male and female he created them.

—Genesis 1:26–27 NLT

God's creation of humans was the pinnacle of all his work. Human beings are the only things he created that are made in his image, purposefully made to be like him. Of course, we are not *fully* like God—he existed before time began. No one created him. He is a perfect, limitless being. He has attributes that we do not have and cannot attain: He is in control of everything, knows everything, is present everywhere, with the ability to do anything. He is God, and we are not.

But because we are made in God's image, we do reflect some of his attributes: holy, loving, just, good, merciful, gracious, faithful, truthful, patient, and wise. We can't live up to this list perfectly, but because we reflect God's image and have his Spirit in us, empowering us, we can live out these characteristics in our broken world.

The concept of "image" is pivotal to identity. When we think of "image," we likely think of the external—who we are to the outside world, our physical appearance, or what we look like in a mirror. We can be tempted to create whatever image we think we want or whatever image we think others want.

Being made in God's image means we are like him. We are not like the image we have of ourselves in our own minds or what the world thinks we should be. I will repeat this phrase again and again: We do not create our identity; we discover it. We may want to create the perfect image of who we think we can and should be. But our identity is what it is because God made us in his image, and we are on a discovery journey to know and understand what that means. Because the Bible is true, we can trust it to tell us who we are.

All people, regardless of race, religion, gender, or ability, are made in God's image. Because of this, all people have dignity and worth. We do not earn our worth through our career, performance, physical ability, or intelligence. It's not about how big our house is, how many houses we have, or whether we even have a place to lay our head. God determines our worth because he created us in his image. We do not have to—and can't—earn it.

This impacts how we treat ourselves. We respect our minds and bodies, as they are given to us by God. We love ourselves, despite our flaws and failures. We steward our lives with intentionality and purpose because we are valuable and have a responsibility to reflect God's image to our broken world.

Speaking of responsibility, this impacts how we treat others too. We have dignity and respect for all people, because they are made in the image of God, just like us. We have a responsibility as image-bearers to care for others, regardless of what they believe about God. We are to see others through the eyes of Jesus and treat them as he would.

Throughout the rest of our lives, God will transform us more and more into his image (Col. 3:10). Jesus is the image of God (Col. 1:15), as are we. Being made in God's image means we are made for relationship because God is relational. In Genesis 1:26 (NLT), we see the communal nature of God: "Let us make human beings in our image." The "us" here is the Trinity: Father, Son, and Holy Spirit. These are distinct personalities, yet all part of God. Community and relationship are at the foundation of being made in God's image. This is God's very nature.

***

"Images are reflections, and that's what we were crafted to be—reflections of God here on earth. We were created to be signposts pointing others to him, mirrors displaying his character to the world. When people see us, they see aspects of God. How amazing! Your purpose, then, isn't something you earn or work for; it's something you already are."

—Elizabeth Garn, *Freedom to Flourish*[6]

I am chosen.

All praise to God, the Father of our Lord Jesus Christ, who has blessed us with every spiritual blessing in the heavenly realms because we are united with Christ. Even before he made the world, God loved us and chose us in Christ to be holy and without fault in his eyes.

—Ephesians 1:3–4 NLT

Before God made the world, he knew he would create human beings that he could love and reveal himself to, so he could have a relationship with them. That includes you! He enjoys you, loves you, knows you, and chose you.

God does not make mistakes. He cannot change, so he won't change his mind about you. He does not ever regret loving you, fighting for you, or drawing you back to himself again and again. God longs to be with his people. This is why he created us: for fellowship with himself. He draws his people to himself because of his deep love and desire to be united with his people (John 6:44). If we come to him, he will not turn us away (John 6:37).

Have you ever been in a group of people, waiting to be selected for a team or game of some sort? It is nerve-wracking, standing there while the captains look over the crowd with scrutiny. With God, we are never on the sidelines, waiting to be chosen. We are seen and known. We are in the game. He has not rejected us. He has a significant work for each of us to be a part of in this world (Eph. 2:10). He gives us good gifts and leads us into places and seasons where we can use those for his glory and the good of others.

My friend Bethany has a long history of wrestling with the idea that she is wanted. She has a deep desire to feel connected to others, but for much of her life, she could not shake the feeling of being left out or unwanted by groups of friends. One day, while processing this ache in her heart, the Lord impressed on her the reality that she is already a valued and highly desired member of a group: the community of the Father, the Son, and the Holy Spirit. God made it clear to her that he chose her to be part of this very important group. They are always happy to see her, and they miss her when she is not drawing near!

While we are chosen on an individual basis, we are with others who are also chosen. Together, we make up the kingdom of God—a beautiful, unique, diverse group of people. God is not discriminatory in his selection, choosing only people of a certain ethnicity, background, gender, or ability. Someday, believers from every nation, tribe, people, and language will stand before God (Rev. 7:9), all made in his image and likeness, representing his beauty. Being a part of his kingdom on earth is a sliver of what we will experience with God someday, for all of eternity.

We do not get a say in who is chosen or who is "fit" for the kingdom. God decides, and he does not play favorites. Throughout the gospels, we read of Jesus eating, conversing with, and healing those that society looked down upon. He crossed ethnic, gender, and socioeconomic lines to reach out to all kinds of people. This is the scandal of grace—that no one deserves the grace we are given, yet anyone can have it.

Is there a person in your life who is hard to love? Someone who irritates you and gets under your skin? How would your attitude, motivation, and behavior look toward that person if you saw them as God sees them? These hard-to-love people are loved deeply by God. He looks at them the way he looks at you—with love, hope, and potential. He sees their brokenness and their need for grace. Do you see it too?

***

"The world tells you many lies about who you are, and you simply have to be realistic enough to remind yourself of this. Every time you feel hurt, offended, or rejected, you have to dare to say to yourself: 'These feelings, strong as they may be, are not telling me the truth about myself. The truth, even though I cannot feel it right now, is that I am the chosen child of God, precious in God's eyes, called the Beloved from all eternity, and held safe in an everlasting embrace.'"

—Henri J.M. Nouwen, *Life of the Beloved*[7]

2

I am an eternal being.

God exists outside of time. No one created him. He has always existed and always will. Psalm 102 says:

> In the beginning you laid the foundations of the earth, and the heavens are the work of your hands. They will perish, but you remain; they will all wear out like a garment. Like clothing you will change them and they will be discarded. But you remain the same, and your years will never end. (Ps. 102:25–27)

He also created his people to live forever, either with him or without him. He gives us the choice, but either way, we exist forever. For the believer, we will experience true satisfaction, joy, and life when we pass on from this earthly life and are in complete union with God in the afterlife.

Our lives are more than just our time on earth. We get so wrapped up in dreams and goals and fulfilling family obligations and making the right career moves and finishing house renovations that it's easy to forget we are meant for more than this earthly life. Our true home is with God, and we'll be with him for all eternity.

The book of Ecclesiastes shines a spotlight on the brevity of life. This book is not for the faint of heart. It is real and honest. It begins with a version of the phrase "everything is meaningless." Solomon, the son of King David, wrote this book of wisdom that raises our eyes to see more than just what is in front of us. We could get everything we ever wanted, but we'll never be satisfied with it. God is the only thing that satisfies. And he has created us in his image with this desire. He has set eternity in our hearts (Eccles. 3:11). We are made in his image, and we reflect a desire for more than this life. C.S. Lewis famously wrote in his book *Mere Christianity*: "If I find in myself desires which nothing in this world can satisfy, the only logical explanation is that I was made for another world."[1] We are made for another world, one that is perfect and good and right. One where we will experience true satisfaction and life everlasting.

Because we are eternal, we must be careful not to find our identity in temporary things. Our careers, bank accounts, even our marriage status will not last beyond our years here on earth. It is so easy to make these things the most important in our lives. We see them, think about them, worry about them every day. But throughout the New Testament, God's people are encouraged to focus not on the temporary but on the eternal. We store up treasures in heaven (1 Tim. 6:18–19), and we keep our eyes on future glory and not on our present troubles (2

Cor. 4:16–17), holding on to hope for a future reward in heaven (Matt. 5:11–12). We need our fellow brothers and sisters to remind us of these truths when life is frustrating.

Below is a passage from Henri J.M. Nouwen's book *Finding My Way Home*. In it, we begin to see how our eternal nature impacts our identity:

> Jesus came to share his identity with you and to tell you that you are the Beloved Sons and Daughters of God. Just for a moment try to enter this enormous mystery that you, like Jesus, are the beloved daughter or the beloved son of God. This is the truth. Furthermore, your belovedness preceded your birth. You were the beloved before your father, mother, brother, sister, or church loved you or hurt you. You are the beloved because you belong to God from all eternity.
>
> God loved you before you were born, and God will love you after you die. In Scripture, God says, 'I have loved you with an everlasting love' (Jer. 31:3, JB). This is a very fundamental truth of your identity. This is who you are whether you feel it or not. You belong to God from eternity to eternity. Life is just a little opportunity for you during a few years to say, 'I love you, too.'"[2]

Your belovedness preceded your birth! That means from before you existed, you were beloved. From the moment you existed, you were beloved. And you will spend eternity with Jesus in this beloved relationship.

In this section, we focus on our eternal nature: We are citizens of heaven, we are co-heirs with Christ, we are God's inheritance, we are alive, and we are protected.

I am a citizen of heaven.

But we are citizens of heaven, where the Lord Jesus Christ lives. And we are eagerly waiting for him to return as our Savior. He will take our weak mortal bodies and change them into glorious bodies like his own, using the same power with which he will bring everything under his control.

—Philippians 3:20–21 NLT

When we become a part of God's family, we no longer belong to the world; we belong to Christ. We are his, and he is ours. We no longer make our way through this world as though this is the only life we have. We realize we are made for eternal life, and we start to live with an eternal focus. Our primary identity as a citizen is no longer to our city, state, or country. We are citizens of the kingdom of God, living for eternity.

God has set eternity in the hearts of men (Eccles. 3:11), that we might long for a place that is truly our home. This will be an eternal home spent with him and those who have gone before us, where we will experience life as it was meant to be. As citizens of heaven, we live in this broken world now with great hope—not in political systems, how much money we have in the bank, or in our work ethic. We live with a deep-seated hope in Jesus, who is coming again to make all things new, including us and our world.

While we look forward to this reality, we can't live in ignorance of the world we are living in right now. No matter how broken and dark the world is, our life here and now matters greatly. We still need to steward our lives well, and how we do that is impacted by being a citizen of the kingdom of God. We care about our family, neighbors, coworkers, and others in our lives. We feed the hungry, serve the sick, fight for the oppressed, and help the poor. Being a citizen of heaven impacts our future, but it also impacts the way we live our lives now:

> Above all, you must live as citizens of heaven, conducting yourselves in a manner worthy of the Good News about Christ. Then, whether I come and see you again or only hear about you, I will know that you are standing together with one spirit and one purpose, fighting together for the faith, which is the Good News. Don't be intimidated in any way by your enemies. This will be a sign to them that they are going to be destroyed, but that you are going to be saved, even by God himself. For you have been given not only the privilege of trusting in Christ but also the privilege of suffering for him. We are in this struggle together. You have seen my struggle in the past, and you know that I am still in the midst of it. (Phil. 1:27–30 NLT)

Paul connects living as citizens of heaven with living our lives in a manner "worthy of the Good News." We are to be united together with our brothers and sisters in Christ. We may experience opposition, but we need not fear those who can kill the body but cannot kill the soul (Matt. 10:28). We stand together, we fight together, and we struggle together. This passage does not emphasize individuality but unity and community. We need one another to live as citizens of heaven.

In Ephesians 4:1–3, Paul again speaks of living a life worthy of our calling: to be humble, gentle, and patient with each other, being gracious with others because of our love for them. We try our hardest to stay unified in the Spirit because we are bound by peace. Again, there is a theme of togetherness, not individuality. We are so inclined to think of our identity in Christ only as personal and private. While it is personal, it is also communal. What a witness it would be to the world to choose good over greed, to choose people over profit. We do not hustle for more and more because we have all we need stored up for us as treasure in heaven (Matt. 6:20).

This world is not our home. The way we live our lives will look foreign to the outside world. But as we live in this world together with other believers—fellow foreigners in a strange land—we are reminded to live with eternity on our minds:

> Since you have been raised to new life with
> Christ, set your sights on the realities of heaven,

where Christ sits in the place of honor at God's right hand. Think about the things of heaven, not the things of earth. For you died to this life, and your real life is hidden with Christ in God. And when Christ, who is your life, is revealed to the whole world, you will share in all his glory. (Col. 3:1–4 NLT)

***

"Christians are, indeed, citizens of God's heavenly city, but these citizens are always the best possible citizens of their earthly city. They walk in the steps of the One who laid down his life for his opponents."

—Timothy Keller, *Center Church: Doing Balanced, Gospel-Centered Ministry in Your City*[3]

I am a co-heir with Christ.

Praise be to the God and Father of our Lord Jesus Christ! In his great mercy he has given us new birth into a living hope through the resurrection of Jesus Christ from the dead, and into an inheritance that can never perish, spoil or fade. This inheritance is kept in heaven for you, who through faith are shielded by God's power until the coming of the salvation that is ready to be revealed in the last time.

—1 Peter 1:3–5

As members of the family of God and a brother or sister to Christ, we are co-heirs with him. An heir receives an inheritance. This is not an inheritance like the world gives—a house, a business, money, or possessions. Our inheritance is to experience God forever, with the family of believers, as we live eternally.

As we are adopted by God into his family, which is a legal change in status, we also become co-heirs with Christ. As in all adoptions, there is a legal entitlement to any inheritance that a parent has to give. An adopted child is not treated as a separate category, but as a full-fledged member of the family.

Not only do we not receive the punishment we deserve for our sin (death), but we receive an eternal inheritance in heaven. This is what makes the gospel powerful and unbelievable! God does not just leave us morally neutral, free from sin's power and penalty, and in right standing with him. We are given so much more. Romans 8 explains this idea through the example of a slave becoming a son:

> For those who are led by the Spirit of God are the children of God. The Spirit you received does not make you slaves, so that you live in fear again; rather, the Spirit you received brought about your adoption to sonship. And by him we cry, "Abba, Father." The Spirit himself testifies with our spirit that we are God's children. Now if we are children, then we are heirs—heirs of God and co-heirs with Christ, if indeed we share in his sufferings in order that we may also share in his glory. (Rom. 8:14–17)

Not only are we not slaves, we are heirs! Talk about a role reversal. We are not slaves to people-pleasing, pride, or perfectionism. We are not bound by our addictions or burdened by our brokenness. We are free men and women who will receive good gifts from our Father. We have been named, called, and counted as the children of God.

The Spirit testifies that we are his children, and if we are his children, we are heirs. While we share in this inheritance, we also share in the sufferings of Christ. Being a child of God does not mean our lives will be perfect and peaceful. But it does mean that God is with us throughout the circumstances of life, and that we can cling to the promises he gives us in his Word.

We are heirs to an inheritance that will never perish, spoil, or fade, kept in heaven for us. Collectively, we are all heirs together as God's children. God doesn't play favorites. His inheritance doesn't run out. We are united together in Christ, with no one being superior or inferior:

> For you are all children of God through faith in Christ Jesus. And all who have been united with Christ in baptism have put on Christ, like putting on new clothes. There is no longer Jew or Gentile, slave or free, male and female. For you are all one in Christ Jesus. And now that you belong to Christ, you are the true children of Abraham. You are his heirs, and God's promise to Abraham belongs to you. (Gal. 3:26–29 NLT)

To be elevated to the status of co-heir with Christ feels almost disrespectful toward him. Who are we to have this title? But this is the reality of our identity. To say we are not an heir would be to say Christ is not an heir. And to say we have a claim to an inheritance without Christ would be a lie. The only thing we inherit without Christ is eternal death. With Christ, we inherit eternal life.

***

"Not all the outward forms on earth,
Nor rites that God has given,
Nor will of man, nor blood, nor birth,
Can raise a soul to Heaven!
The Sovereign will of God alone
Creates us heirs of Grace—
Born in the image of His Son,
A new peculiar race.
The Spirit, like some heavenly wind
Blows on the sons of flesh.
Creates a new—a heavenly mind—
And forms the man afresh."

—C.H. Spurgeon, from a sermon entitled "Restless!
Peaceless!"[4]

I am God's inheritance.

What joy for the nation whose God is the LORD,
whose people he has chosen as his inheritance.

—Psalm 33:12 NLT

In Genesis 15, God makes a promise to Abraham: He will become the father of many nations. These nations would become God's inheritance, his chosen people. But in his old age, Abraham didn't have any children, and he questioned this news from God. He only had a servant, so how could he have any heirs if he had no children? God tells him that he will have a son who will become his heir and that the descendants of Abraham will be as numerous as the stars (Gen. 15:5). And as the Israelites were rescued out of Egypt, and given the promised land, God showed them they were "his very own people and his special possession" (Deut. 4:20 NLT).

We are also God's treasured possession. We are formed by him in our mother's womb (Jer. 1:5) and chosen and adopted as his children (Eph. 1:4–5). We are God's inheritance. We are his sons and daughters, part of his family forever. The nations are his inheritance (Ps. 82:8), the people of his pasture as he leads the flock (Ps. 95:7).

When we trust Christ for our salvation, we get so many benefits. And best of all, we get God himself. We get a relationship with him that is secure and unwavering. We get unconditional, unfailing love. We are able to know him and experience his presence. This is a familial relationship that is never lost or severed.

These things are an incredible, unbelievable benefit to us that we do not earn and don't deserve. Astoundingly, God gets something out of this deal as well: He gets us. He gets a family to care for and love. He gets to spend eternity with us. He gets our love, however imperfect and lacking it may be. He gets glory as we offer up lives that honor him. God is pleased with our reconciliation to him because he receives the inheritance of a relationship with his children. We are his people, belonging to him. It is almost unbelievable that God would choose us and love us and invest in us as his inheritance, but he does. This is how much he loves his children, whom he has created and called to himself. He took a chance on us, not forcing us to love him but allowing us the choice to love and follow him. Every time we make that choice, he rejoices.

In his letter to the church in Ephesus, Paul writes:

> I have not stopped thanking God for you. I pray for you constantly, asking God, the glorious Father of our Lord Jesus Christ, to give you spiritual wisdom and insight so that you might grow in your knowledge of God. I pray that your hearts will be flooded with light so that you can understand the confident hope he has given to

those he called—his holy people who are his rich and glorious inheritance. (Eph. 1:16–18 NLT)

We are God's inheritance, not because of how great we are, but because he loves us and has made us a part of his family. And all across the world, God's children are his inheritance. His kingdom is not bound by borders, languages, ethnicities, or mental ability. God's inheritance is not bound by time; it is past, present, and future. We are part of a family that lives on forever.

What is our response to this reality? We are not God's people because we keep the rules. We do not obey to get love. We are loved, and so we obey. It's not an automatic response; we still have a choice. But the more we reflect on and internalize the depth of God's love for us, and the reality that we will be his people no matter what, the more we experience transformation in our lives and grow in godliness. Paul describes this transformation:

> For the grace of God has appeared that offers salvation to all people. It teaches us to say "No" to ungodliness and worldly passions, and to live self-controlled, upright and godly lives in this present age, while we wait for the blessed hope—the appearing of the glory of our great God and Savior, Jesus Christ, who gave himself for us to redeem us from all wickedness and to purify for himself a people that are his very own, eager to do what is good. (Titus 2:11–14)

***

When you see people, you say "beloved."
The lost and lonely are found and free.
A city broken is not forsaken.
Our eyes are opened to see You again.
You will have Your inheritance.

—Miracle City Church, *Inheritance*[5]

I am no longer dead but alive.

As for you, you were dead in your transgressions and sins
. . . But because of his great love for us, God, who is rich in
mercy, made us alive with Christ even when we were dead
in transgressions—it is by grace you have been saved. And
God raised us up with Christ and seated us with him in the
heavenly realms in Christ Jesus, in order that in the coming
ages he might show the incomparable riches of his grace, ex-
pressed in his kindness to us in Christ Jesus.

—Ephesians 2:1, 4–7

Throughout Scripture, we learn we are dead to sin and
selfish ambitions, and we are alive in Christ. This is a
foundational truth for believers! Because of our sin, we
are destined for death. Adam and Eve, before they ate
the fruit of the tree of the knowledge of good and evil,
had eternal life. By disobeying God, they introduced
death into the world. They would no longer live with
God forever.

But God, in his great mercy, provides his son Jesus
as a perfect sacrifice for our sins. Jesus took the punishment we deserved (death) so that we might live.
Through Adam, we were destined for death, and
through Christ, we now live (1 Cor. 15:22).

This does not just mean eternal life after we experience a physical death, but it also means we are spiritually alive now on earth. When we have died to sin, we no longer continue to live in it. We have the power to overcome. Romans 6:1–11 is packed with truth about this new nature of ours. Throughout these eleven verses, Paul uses the word "power" six times! He is highlighting the fact that Jesus was raised from the dead by the power of God (Rom. 6:4) and by that same power, sin has no hold over us.

Christianity is the only religion across the world with a leader who died, came back to life, and is still living today. All religions worship their founders, but Christians worship a God who is still alive. And because Jesus rose from the dead, God can resurrect all kinds of dead things. Yes, someday in heaven, but also now. Dead dreams. Broken lives. Burned bridges. God restores broken things and makes them new. I've seen him do it. It's not easy. It might take a long time. We may not see restoration until heaven. But the possibilities for God to breathe new life into all kinds of dead and broken things are immense.

The way we experience this new life that Jesus offers us is through the Holy Spirit. We don't just try harder to get free from the unhealthy patterns in our lives. We don't "white knuckle it" with willpower until we rid ourselves of the anger, jealousy, hate, pride, or myriad of other things we deal with.

It is through the Spirit that we experience this new life. Romans 8 explains that it is the power of the life-giving Spirit that frees us from the power of sin (Rom.

8:2). We, in our weakness, were never able to overcome sin, so Jesus came in a body like ours to bring an end to sin's control over us (Rom. 8:3). We are no longer controlled by our selfish nature but are controlled by the Spirit (Rom. 8:9) and Christ living within us (Rom. 8:10). And just as Jesus was raised from the dead, so will we be raised, by this same Spirit living in us (Rom. 8:11).

Before Christ, we were dead in sin. After Christ, we are dead *to* sin and alive *in* Christ—free from the punishment and power of sin. This is true for us individually and corporately. The body of Christ is spiritually alive. Together, we can be led by the Spirit who moves in our individual hearts at the same time.

The early church in Acts was marked by this reality. Throughout the book, we read about the Spirit moving powerfully in the midst of the apostles as they preached the gospel, and the church increased in number (Acts 9:31). On the day of Pentecost, the Holy Spirit was poured out, not on individuals sitting at home alone, but in the place where they had gathered together (Acts 2:1–4). When we hear reports of revival in churches and colleges, the Spirit is at work in powerful ways within the body of believers. May we experience being alive through the Spirit individually and collectively in order to experience life the way God meant it to be.

***

"Christ was sent not to mend wounded people or wake sleepy people or advise confused people or inspire bored people or spur on lazy people or educate ignorant people, but to raise dead people."

—Dane C. Ortlund, *Gentle and Lowly*[6]

I am protected.

If God is for us, who can be against us?

—Romans 8:31

Before we came to Christ, we were dead in our sins, belonging to the prince of the power of the air (Eph. 2:2). We lived in spiritual darkness. We followed the ways of this world because we didn't know anything different. We did whatever was right in our own eyes. We were predisposed to sin, led by our thoughts and desires of the flesh.

But God, in his mercy, chose to reconcile us to himself. And because of this work, we no longer belong to the ways of this world but to Christ. We go from death to life and rid ourselves of a proclivity to choose darkness. We desire light and truth, even if only in small amounts. We still wrestle with sin to keep it at bay, and we may lose a battle here and there, but victory is ultimately ours. We are no longer enslaved to sin or tripped up by the schemes of the devil. Our names are written in the book of life, and our status as children of God is secure.

We are fighting against an unseen enemy, but we are protected by the blood of Christ and our very testimony of God at work in our lives (Rev. 12:11). We belong to God (1 Cor. 3:23) and do not have to fear what may happen to us. Our forgiveness and redemption are secure in Christ and cannot be lost (Eph. 1:7). We are protected by God because God is powerful. He is our strength and defense (Exod. 15:2). He rules powerfully over kingdoms (2 Chron. 20:6).

God graciously gives us these assurances. The end of Romans 8 also reminds us how secure we are in Christ:

> Who shall separate us from the love of Christ? Shall trouble or hardship or persecution or famine or nakedness or danger or sword? As it is written: "For your sake we face death all day long; we are considered as sheep to be slaughtered." No, in all these things we are more than conquerors through him who loved us. For I am convinced that neither death nor life, neither angels nor demons, neither the present nor the future, nor any powers, neither height nor depth, nor anything else in all creation, will be able to separate us from the love of God that is in Christ Jesus our Lord. (Rom. 8:35–39)

We will experience opposition and hardship in this life. It's a certainty. We may even suffer persecution or harm because of our faith. But nothing can drive a wedge between us and God.

We are not only protected individually but collectively. I love the imagery of Jesus as our Good Shepherd.

We are the people of God and the sheep of his pasture (Ps. 100:3). The Good Shepherd protects his flock when they are attacked, sacrificing his life for the sheep. We are safe and secure under the watchful eye of the Good Shepherd (John 10:27–30). Even when we walk through the darkest valleys, God walks beside us with comfort and protection (Ps. 23:4). We are stronger together in the flock.

We can take an active role in our protection. In Paul's letter to the church in Ephesus, he encourages them to be strong in the Lord by putting on the full armor of God, which guards us from the schemes of the evil one:

> For our struggle is not against flesh and blood, but against the rulers, against the authorities, against the powers of this dark world and against the spiritual forces of evil in the heavenly realms. Therefore put on the full armor of God, so that when the day of evil comes, you may be able to stand your ground, and after you have done everything, to stand. Stand firm then, with the belt of truth buckled around your waist, with the breastplate of righteousness in place, and with your feet fitted with the readiness that comes from the gospel of peace. In addition to all this, take up the shield of faith, with which you can extinguish all the flaming arrows of the evil one. Take the helmet of salvation and the sword of the Spirit, which is the word of God. And pray in the Spirit on all occasions with all kinds of

prayers and requests. With this in mind, be alert and always keep on praying for all the Lord's people. (Eph. 6:12–18)

The word of God aids us in our fight. It is our offensive weapon, living and active, sharper than any two-edged sword (Heb. 4:12). Combined with prayer, we are using powerful weapons to participate in our protection. And together, our prayers with fellow believers are a light in the darkness. Throughout the book of Acts, we read of the early church praying together and trusting God together. Just like the early church, we are stronger when we are together in the body of Christ.

***

"You are guarded by [God's] power at all times, protecting you from enemy attack. When you feel assaulted in any way—from your circumstances, from your own mind, or from invisible spiritual forces of evil—call forth the truth that you are seated with Christ in the heavenly realms. In this seat, you wear the armor of God."

—Heather Holleman, *Seated with Christ*[7]

3

I am being transformed.

God never changes, yet he changes us. He knows the depths of our brokenness and our inability to pick ourselves up by our bootstraps to save ourselves. He also knows our full potential, even when we can't see it.

God transforms us through his Spirit and through renewing our minds (Rom. 12:2). We renew our minds by replacing the lies we've been told about our identity with the truth—who God says we are. We believe this truth by faith and live it out through the Spirit. We aren't just transformed into whatever we want, but we are transformed into the likeness of God through Christ (Eph. 4:23–24).

We can't manufacture transformation. We can't just try to behave better by our own willpower. We need the power of God to live as new creations. God both desires for us to grow and gives us the things we need to do so. It is through abiding in him that we bear good fruit (John 15). We don't control what we produce; God transforms us as we walk in step with him. God is more concerned with who we are becoming than what we do for him. As someone who is tempted to believe she can earn love, acceptance, and approval from others by doing good things, this is great news.

Two theological words come to mind when I think about transformation. The first is justification. When we come to Christ, we are accepted because of his sacrifice on the cross on our behalf. We believe in him through faith, and we are justified, or made right with God, through faith (Rom. 5:1). This is not because of any good things we could have done but because of what Jesus has done on the cross. Justification is God's work alone.

The second word that comes to mind is sanctification. This term simply means the process of being made holy. This happens throughout the rest of our lives as we walk with Christ. God doesn't expect us to immediately think and act perfectly once we trust him for eternal life. Sanctification happens little by little and is work we join God in. At some point in our lives, we will experience temptation, trials, and suffering. These things help form us into the image of Christ.

As we develop an intimate relationship with God, our awareness of our brokenness grows too. We start to want the things of God instead of the selfish desires of our heart. Throughout the rest of our lives, we continue to submit ourselves to God, and he continues to transform us. Justification is a one-time event, while sanctification is a lifelong process. We are washed clean, sanctified, and justified in the name of Jesus and through the

Spirit (1 Cor. 6:11). We are no longer our former, false self, but a new creation.

This new creation is the goal of transformation. While we are made in God's likeness (Gen. 1:26), we are sinful from the moment we're born. Jesus came to earth in human likeness to pay for our sin (Rom. 8:3). Jesus made himself nothing, being made in human likeness, so that he could take our place on the cross (Phil. 2:7–8). When God looks at us, he sees the righteousness of Christ. He transforms us into the image of Jesus (Rom. 8:29; 2 Cor. 3:18). It's like we swap likenesses. Christ took on our sin through his human form, and we become righteous through him.

We have a responsibility to work on our own growth, but we don't do it alone. We need the Holy Spirit, and we need other people. In their book *How People Grow*, Dr. Henry Cloud and Dr. John Townsend talk about the role of other people in our growth. While we may want a quick transformation overnight, God often uses other people to mold us into the people he has created us to be. Cloud writes: "Independence from relationship is independence from God himself, for he is present in his Body; it is also independence from the way he designed for us to grow."[1]

When I think of the seasons of deepest growth in my life, each one is marked by people who walked alongside me on my journey. It is in relationships that we get glimpses of God—hearing truth in love, being given grace when we screw up, and experiencing love, understanding, empathy, and acceptance.

While we don't have to clean ourselves up to come to God, he also doesn't leave us where we are in our mess. I am so grateful for that!

In this section, we focus on how God is transforming us: We are forgiven, we are clothed in righteousness, we are set free, we are clay being molded, and we are being healed.

I am forgiven.

This is the message we heard from Jesus and now declare to you: God is light, and there is no darkness in him at all. So we are lying if we say we have fellowship with God but go on living in spiritual darkness; we are not practicing the truth. But if we are living in the light, as God is in the light, then we have fellowship with each other, and the blood of Jesus, his Son, cleanses us from all sin. If we claim we have no sin, we are only fooling ourselves and not living in the truth. But if we confess our sins to him, he is faithful and just to forgive us our sins and to cleanse us from all wickedness. If we claim we have not sinned, we are calling God a liar and showing that his word has no place in our hearts.

—1 John 1:5–10 NLT

Forgiveness through Christ is a foundational truth of the Christian life. We do not earn our forgiveness by doing good works; we are forgiven only through the blood of Jesus Christ (Eph. 1:7). In the Old Testament, priests made sacrifices to please God and pay for the sins of the people. The priests were set apart from the rest of the Israelites, and God required a blood sacrifice for the forgiveness of sins (Heb. 9:22). Only the priests had access to God, and only the priests could present the sacrifices as an offering to the Lord.

Jesus changed all of this. We no longer need special people who are set apart with exclusive access to come into God's presence and satisfy the payment for sin. Jesus has served as the ultimate sacrifice. He is the ultimate mediator (1 Tim. 2:5), the great high priest (Heb. 4:14), and we have access to God through him (Heb. 10:19).

Forgiveness isn't earned, but it also isn't passive. Our role in forgiveness is to acknowledge our wrongdoings, confess it to God, and trust by faith that we are forgiven. We are forgiven when we ask God to forgive us. This involves agreeing with God about what our sin is. The Holy Spirit works in our hearts and minds to convict us of our shortcomings, and we bring that reality to the cross. The Greek word for forgiveness used in 1 John 1:9 (*aphiemi*) means "to let go."[2] This is what we do with our sins at the cross: We let them go, God lets them go, and we pick up forgiveness. God blots out our transgressions and does not remember our mistakes (Heb. 8:12).

As our faith grows, so does our awareness of our sin. We may find that we sin *less*, but we'll never be sinless. (Some of us may feel like we sin *more*, because we're more aware of how messed up we are!) We never "arrive" in the Christian life. There won't ever be a point when we don't need forgiveness.

Pastor and author Tim Keller once said, "The gospel is not just the ABCs of the Christian life but the A to Z of the Christian life."[3] We never graduate from needing the gospel; we need it moment by moment. The gospel is this: No matter how flawed and sinful and broken we are, we have a Savior that much greater who died for our sins to give us eternal life.

We cannot consider forgiveness without also considering sin. But we should not be consumed with our brokenness to the point that it hinders our belief in our forgiveness through Christ. Sometimes, believing we are forgiven is a choice we have to make, despite our feelings. There is no guilt, punishment, or condemnation for those who belong to Christ Jesus (Rom. 8:1). He did not come into this world to condemn the world but to save it (John 3:17). Unfortunately, Christ followers, ourselves included, are imperfect. At times we are hurtful. We are people who judge and condemn others. Do not let the voices of a few crowd out the voice of God that speaks truth: *You are forgiven.*

In Matthew 6, as Jesus is preaching the Sermon on the Mount, he talks about our attitude in prayer. He encourages his followers to ask God to forgive them as they have forgiven others. We ask God to forgive us, plural, not just singular.

When we internalize and believe the depths to which we have been forgiven, we can't help but forgive others. Experiencing our own forgiveness changes us from the inside out. If a perfect and holy God can look past the sins of his people and love us, we can love others. As God is quick to forgive us, we are to be quick to forgive. This doesn't mean we don't hold others accountable or that there aren't consequences to sin. But we don't hold grudges or bitterness toward others who wrong us.

How we view forgiveness impacts how we live. God is "gracious and compassionate, slow to anger and rich in love" (Ps. 145:8). Because we are made in his image and are being transformed by him in the likeness of his Son, we are also to be gracious, compassionate, patient, and loving toward others.

***

"To be a Christian means to forgive the inexcusable because God has forgiven the inexcusable in you."

—C.S. Lewis, *The Weight of Glory*[4]

I am clothed in righteousness.

I no longer count on my own righteousness through obeying the law; rather, I become righteous through faith in Christ. For God's way of making us right with himself depends on faith.

—Philippians 3:9 NLT

In Luke 18, Jesus tells his disciples a parable of the Pharisee and the tax collector. Both men go to the temple to pray. The Pharisee prays with a heart of pride and self-righteousness, considering himself better than the sinners around him. The tax collector prays with a heart of humility, asking for mercy. Jesus explained that the tax collector went home justified before God, for "those who exalt themselves will be humbled, and those who humble themselves will be exalted" (Luke 18:14).

The Pharisees got their confidence from obeying the Jewish laws. They looked down on everyone else because they thought themselves to be the most righteous and religious people.

But we know that we are not made righteous by how we pray, how much we give, how often we read our Bible, or how little we sin. Whether we've been the prodigal son who runs from his good father, or the elder brother whose prideful heart gets in the way, while we were still sinners, Christ died for us (Rom. 5:8). Because of that, we are now made right with God through faith. We do not keep the rules to get on God's good side. The rules, called "the law" in the New Testament, won't save us. The law shows us our true reality: We can never keep it perfectly, but we don't need to. Jesus did that. The work to live the perfect life has already been completed on the cross.

Despite your past, present, or future, today you stand righteous before God. This incredible reality means we have a new self to live out—a self that is righteous in the eyes of God. Galatians 3 explains what this looks like: "For you are all children of God through faith in Christ Jesus. And all who have been united with Christ in baptism have put on Christ, like putting on new clothes. There is no longer Jew or Gentile, slave or free, male and female. For you are all one in Christ Jesus" (Gal. 3:26–28 NLT).

Baptism is a symbol of our death to our old life and our rebirth into new life in Christ, trusting in him for salvation. In this new life, we can now "wear Christ." His righteousness is imputed to us, as though it were our own. Forgiveness of our sins makes us morally neutral with God, and yet he goes a step further to say we are *righteous*—in right standing with him.

How would your day-to-day life look if you believed you were clothed in righteousness? What if your standing with God didn't depend on your ability to be nice to others and do the right thing?

In my life, this truth leads to more peace and joy. I'm an anxious person by nature, but knowing I stand in the truth of being made right in God's sight, not through my abilities, but through my faith in Jesus's ability to live a perfect life, makes all the difference. I experience peace! I don't need to run on pride or prove myself to others. I experience the joy of being loved and accepted instead of never knowing where I stand with God. Scripture says:

> I am overwhelmed with joy in the LORD my God! For he has dressed me with the clothing of salvation and draped me in a robe of righteousness. I am like a bridegroom dressed for his wedding or a bride with her jewels. (Isa. 61:10 NLT)

Being clothed in righteousness allows us to put off the things in Colossians 3:5–11: the earthly things lurking within you like impurity, lust, evil desires, greed, idolatry, anger, rage, malicious behavior, slander, and dirty language.

As Colossians 3:7 explains, we used to do these things when we were a part of this world. But once we come to Christ, he wipes away our old nature. We can put on our new nature, and "be renewed as you learn to know your Creator and become like him. In this new life, it doesn't matter if you are a Jew or a Gentile, circumcised or uncircumcised, barbaric, uncivilized, slave, or free. Christ is all that matters, and he lives in all of us" (Col. 3:10–11 NLT).

In this new nature, this new way of life, we put on (clothe ourselves with) the things of Colossians 3:12–15: compassion, kindness, humility, gentleness, patience, forgiveness, love, peace, and thankfulness. Through the righteousness of Christ, we are able to display these characteristics just as God does. We are made in his image, and while we still falter and fail because of our imperfections, we are still righteous in his sight through Jesus.

What does it mean that together, we are all clothed in righteousness? We are all shopping at the same clothing store. No one is given more righteousness by God than another, for we have all fallen short and stand in need of a Savior. There is no need for comparison and no place for jealousy. The righteousness of God is given as a garment to each of his children to wear—and because someone else wears it does not mean we cannot. God's righteousness through Jesus will never run out.

***

"It is the most counterintuitive aspect of Christianity, that we are declared right with God not once we begin to get our act together but once we collapse into honest acknowledgment that we never will."

—Dane C. Ortlund, *Deeper*[5]

I am set free.

To the Jews who had believed him, Jesus said, "If you hold
to my teaching, you are really my disciples. Then you will
know the truth, and the truth will set you free." They
answered him, "We are Abraham's descendants and have
never been slaves of anyone. How can you say that we shall
be set free?" Jesus replied, "Very truly I tell you, everyone
who sins is a slave to sin. Now a slave has no permanent
place in the family, but a son belongs to it forever. So if the
Son sets you free, you will be free indeed."

—John 8:31–36

Sin enslaves us. It is alluring, enticing, and can become
all-encompassing. It is subtle and sneaky, ensnaring us
when we least expect it.

But Jesus, who had no sin, became sin for us (2 Cor.
5:21). He took the penalty (death) and died on the cross
for us. We will never be perfect, like Jesus was. We will
always deal with our own brokenness and mistakes until we are perfected in heaven. But the power of sin has
been broken by Jesus. We can be set free from the hold
it has over us.

Jesus makes the point in this passage that a slave is
not truly a member of the family. A slave works to earn
his or her place in the system. He is not a child; he's an

employee of sorts. This is not how God sees us. We are his children, and in being a part of his family, we are set free from working for his love and favor and acceptance. We do not have to earn our keep. We are not kicked out when we make mistakes. We have the security of knowing we are in his family forever. We are also free from things like people-pleasing, perfectionism, and performing.

Further into John 8, the Jews again bring up their identity as sons of Abraham. They are not understanding the connection Jesus is making to God as their Father. Their identity is in the wrong person, Abraham, versus their true Father (John 8:39–42). We do not set our identity in our earthly family connection, like the Jews. Our identity is in our spiritual family, and all that God promises us.

Jesus also brings up another father of theirs: the father of lies (John 8:44). This father, the devil, does not want us to be free in Christ. He wants us to believe the lies of this world: that what we want deep in our hearts will satisfy us more than Jesus will and that we deserve total freedom from all rules or responsibilities because we can and should do whatever we want.

The freedom Jesus offers doesn't mean there are no boundaries or responsibilities. We are not accepted by God because we obey his teachings, but it's through his teachings that we are set free to love and serve him and others with no conditions. In John 8:31, Jesus explains to the Jews that they must hold to the teachings of Jesus to know the truth, and it's that truth that will set them free.

To hold to his teachings, we abide in his Word. Abiding leads to obedience. We are free to obey. It sounds counterintuitive, right? If I'm free, why would I obey? Can't I do whatever I want because there's grace to cover it anyway? We obey because we love. The ultimate example of giving up freedom to be obedient took place when Jesus gave up his life and went to the cross to die. He laid down his life willingly, in obedience to the Father.

As a community of Christ followers, we are set free together. We don't live under the law, so why would we expect others to do so? We are not to put religious expectations on others. We are free from seeking approval from one another, and we are free to love one another unconditionally, with no expectations.

About once a month, I lead worship at my local Celebrate Recovery group—a faith-based recovery program for people experiencing a variety of hurts, habits, and hang-ups. For those who have worked the program, there is often a desire to get involved in the community and give back. A central theme is, "If you've been set free, set others free." There is incredible freedom in sitting with a group of people and addressing an aspect of your life that has become unmanageable. What a relief to talk about something difficult in your life and to hear from someone across the table, "Me too. You can be free." God uses the people around us to help us realize and step into our freedom.

We need each other to remind us of who we are in Christ—that we do not follow the father of lies, the ruler of the world. We are set free from lies. We are set free from a "try harder, do more" rhetoric. We are set free to be transformed into who God has created us to be.

***

"While I don't for one second think we can earn God's grace by checking off a to-do list, I do believe that there is liberation in obedience. When we live like Jesus, when we take his teachings seriously and apply them to life, we don't have to wait until we die to experience freedom from sin. We experience it every day as each step of faith and every good work loosens the chains of sin around our feet."

—Rachel Held Evans, *Faith Unraveled*[6]

I am clay being molded.

Yet you, LORD, are our Father.
We are the clay, you are the potter;
we are all the work of your hand.

—Isaiah 64:8

Have you ever tried to make anything out of clay using a potter's wheel? The process is mesmerizing, as careful hands shape the formless clay into something useful. Over and over, the hands work the clay, and eventually, we see a bowl, a vase, or a mug take shape.

We are created by God, uniquely and wonderfully made (Ps. 139:14). We are created for good works (Eph. 2:10). We are a treasure in which God sees potential (1 Cor. 2:9). God wants to continue to mold us as we follow him. He desires to be at work in our lives, transforming us into the likeness of his Son (Rom. 8:29). This transformation takes time and repetition, like the clay on the potter's wheel.

God uses all kinds of things in our lives to grow us into the people he created us to be. He prunes us with intentionality (John 15:2). He disciplines us because he loves us (Prov. 3:11–12). He refines our hearts like silver and gold (Zech. 13:9). We should treat ourselves with patience and grace, as this process of transformation (sanctification) is lifelong. It doesn't happen overnight when we place our faith in Christ.

It is slow and meaningful work. At times, he molds us through suffering, pain, and trials. In these moments, it can be easy to question God and his intentions. Sometimes, we want to refuse to be shaped. But he, the potter, is greater than the clay (Isa. 29:16). The clay does not say to the potter, "This is how you need to make me." We have no place to demand that God shape us a certain way. We are made by God and formed by his hand; we are not to question why or tell him he's wrong (Rom. 9:20).

Clay on a potter's wheel needs a potter. The clay cannot mold itself, and as such, we cannot create our own identity. It's a discovery of who God desires us to be. It is incredible that he cares enough about us to patiently mold us.

At times, a potter will use great force to mold the clay, and other times, he will make gentle, small adjustments. Over and over, the potter shapes the form. The potter knows what he is working out. He has a vision for the final product. From the beginning, God has formed humans (Gen. 2:7), and he remembers this with compassion (Ps. 103).

I recently found an old social media post between my friend Alyssa and me. In it, she asked me if I felt God was "clumping" or "chiseling" me that day. I replied, "Jack-hammering." While I don't recall the specifics of my answer, isn't that what transformation can feel like sometimes? It can be sharp, surprising, and sustaining.

Collectively, we are all lumps of clay being molded. Some of us are shaped differently than others, with different purposes and plans. Some are shaped quickly, while others take longer. Even though God desires all of us to be representatives of Jesus, we won't all look the same. God allows our unique identities and personalities to shine through. The community of believers will look more like a thrift store shelf of unique mugs and plates and bowls than a nice and neat eight-pack of dinnerware from a big box store.

The benefit of being in a community of clay lumps is that we can empathize with each other when God is working on us. We can encourage and help bear one another's burdens. We can hold each other accountable as we are being transformed by God.

How is God molding and shaping you? How does that feel? It's not always fun to be the lump of clay on the potter's wheel, hands shaping over and over. But how wonderful that the Creator does not leave us as we are, and he is right alongside us as he works.

***

"You see, a potter can only mold the clay when it lies completely in his hand. It requires complete surrender."

—Corrie Ten Boom, *Each New Day*[7]

I am being healed.

Surely he took up our pain and bore our suffering,
yet we considered him punished by God, stricken by him,
and afflicted. But he was pierced for our transgressions, he
was crushed for our iniquities; the punishment that brought
us peace was on him, and by his wounds we are healed. We
all, like sheep, have gone astray, each of us has turned to our
own way; and the Lord has laid on him the iniquity of us all.

—Isaiah 53:4–6

There are numerous prophecies about Jesus in the Old Testament, and this passage from Isaiah 53 is just one, pointing to the punishment Jesus took for us on the cross. He was pierced by the nails in his hands and feet as he was placed on the cross. It is through these wounds he received that we are healed.

We are separated from connection with God because we can't uphold his standards in living a perfect life. Jesus's death on the cross, after living a perfect life we could not, means our connection to God is restored through him. We are saved from death, the punishment for our sin, and are healed through reconciliation to God.

Healing can mean a variety of things. We may first think of it in the context of physical healing. This may happen for us in this life, but it may not. There may be relational, emotional, and mental healing. God desires to take hurting, broken people and make them whole again.

The first thing God does for us regarding our healing is to connect us back to him, restoring our relationship. If this were the only thing God did for us, it would be enough. But he doesn't stop there. He can make broken things new again. He restores things and people to wholeness.

Throughout the gospels, we read eyewitness accounts of miraculous healings by Jesus: the bleeding woman (Mark 5), a paralyzed man (Matt. 9), multiple blind people (Matt. 9; Matt. 20; and John 9, to name a few), as well as leprosy, dropsy, and epilepsy. He even put a man's ear back on his head (Luke 22:51). He brought back Lazarus from the dead, among other people. He bestowed authority on the disciples so they could heal others, and we continue to read about this work in Acts after the Holy Spirit comes.

God can do these same miracles today. We may not see them often, but he can do it and does do it. Sickness, suffering, grief, despair, and pain are ever-present realities in our broken world. While God can and does perform miracles, he may not heal us in the way we would like. I know many people who have a lifelong disability, chronic illness, or physical struggle that has never gone away. It may never go away.

In the midst of these hard things, God offers himself. He brings comfort, hope, and peace. He places us in community where we can experience love and belonging. Often, we are hurt by others in relationships, but we are also healed in relationships with others.

It is powerful to recognize and share our pain with others and to be met with empathy and understanding. Our vulnerability with others brings us into a deeper relationship with them, where we can experience love and acceptance that is a glimpse of what God can give us. When we are in relationship with others, especially those who have experienced the same pain we have, we can experience hope and healing.

There is a reason recovery from addictions and harmful habits is pursued in a group environment. To know we are not alone in our struggles, and that others have found a way through, can be the motivation we need to keep going. As we trust God with these broken places in our lives, he meets us right where we are and helps us walk the road of healing and pursuing wholeness.

***

"As Christians, we confess we are made in the image of the triune God—God in community, you could say. This means that in order for us to flourish as God's image bearers, being with, and belonging to others is necessary. To be in relationship means that we will wound others and we will be wounded by others on some level. It's an unavoidable reality. But the way towards healing is not through individualism—the rejection of community. It's found in a more mature context of belonging. May God lead us to these places, and help us all to grow into greater maturity, so as to be that context—and community—for others."

—Rich Villodas, *Good and Beautiful and Kind*[7]

4

I am connected to God.

At the end of my twenties, I came to the end of my rope. I had been serving in ministry for seven years, and I'd made it my entire identity. If I was doing well at work, I felt great. If I wasn't, I didn't. I felt like I was running on a treadmill and couldn't keep up the pace much longer.

One day, I got off the treadmill. I started a journey inward that hasn't stopped ten years later. As I started to separate my identity from my ministry work, I began to discover for the first time who I was in Christ. I started to build a connection with God that was reminiscent of my college days, when I experienced God as love for the first time.

In this season, I began to just be with God. Not for any certain purpose, but just to enjoy him. It took a while to get to a point where I felt like I was *actually* enjoying him. So much of my relationship with God had been wrapped up in ministry that it was hard to separate. What began in that season of life has continued into a deeper and more meaningful connection with God than I thought possible.

We are all connected to God. He resides within us, making his home in us (John 1:14). He desires for us to make our home in him—the place of true satisfaction and fulfillment for us. We have an incredible promise of eternal life in Christ, but if we miss out on the connection to God here and now, we're missing the whole point.

When I think about our connection to God, I think of John 13–17. This section of Scripture is called the "Farewell Discourse." In it, Jesus spends his last hours with his disciples. He pours his heart out. He washes their feet. He gives them final instructions. He begins his walk to the garden of Gethsemane, knowing that death is coming.

Within these chapters are rich truths about our connection to God. In John 14:6, Jesus calls himself the way, the truth, and the life. He is the way we get to God the Father. He is our connection to God. In him, we find abundant life now and eternal life to come. In verse 16, Jesus introduces the Holy Spirit, explaining that he is our advocate after Jesus departs. In verse 20, Jesus explains that he is in the Father, we are in him, and he is in us. Collectively, Jesus is within us, and we are in him. God is omnipresent, so he can be with and in us—all of us, at all times. Honestly, it's hard to wrap my mind around this reality, how God can be present everywhere, all at once!

Next, Jesus describes the Christian life and our relationship to God using an analogy of a vine and branches (John 15). This is one of my favorite passages of Scripture, and I will share more about that analogy in this section. It describes the way we reside in God and how we draw strength, joy, and life from him.

Of special note in our connection with God is the third member of the Trinity that doesn't get talked about as much as he should: the Holy Spirit. He is distinct from God the Father and Jesus the Son. He cultivates our connection with God, enables us to live the Christian life, and helps us know God and know ourselves. He is our advocate, sent to teach us and remind us of what Jesus has said (John 14:26). He convicts us of sin (John 16:8) and intercedes for us (Rom. 8:26). He is alive in us as the Spirit of truth (John 14:17), setting us free from the law of sin and death (Rom. 8:2) and is with us forever (John 14:16).

Everyone is connected to God through the Holy Spirit, and we are all also connected to one another. The same Spirit fills each believer, all at the same time. We share the same Spirit, and there is plenty of him to go around.

In this section, we focus on the ways we are connected to God: We are filled with the Holy Spirit, we are worshippers, we are temples, we are branches on the vine, and we are creations made to create.

I am filled with the Holy Spirit.

And I will ask the Father, and he will give you another
Advocate, who will never leave you. He is the Holy Spirit,
who leads into all truth. The world cannot receive him,
because it isn't looking for him and doesn't recognize him.
But you know him, because he lives with you now and later
will be in you.

—John 14:16–17 NLT

Jesus tells his disciples in John 14 that it is better if he leaves them and the Holy Spirit comes. But what could be better than having God in the flesh beside you? This truth shows the power and significance of the Spirit. We can experience a closeness with God through the Spirit that was not the same when Jesus walked the earth. God resides in us, through his Spirit.

When we make the decision to trust Christ, we are filled with the Holy Spirit. After that point, we are constantly filled with the Spirit. We don't have to continue to ask to be filled. Often, when my friend Ben speaks to the college students involved in the ministry in which we serve, he reminds them that we don't need to invite the Holy Spirit into our lives. The Spirit is already present. But we do need to continue to walk in step with the Spirit, yielding control to him. When we do this, we are empowered by the Spirit. We are always filled, but we aren't always empowered.

Walking in the power of the Spirit is a moment-by-moment experience. As we go throughout our day, we recognize our missteps, confess them to God, thank him for his forgiveness, and then surrender to the Spirit, letting him lead and guide us throughout our day. By faith, we trust that we are empowered by the Spirit. As we do this, we begin to notice the fruit of the Spirit, which Paul describes in Galatians 5:22–23 (NLT): love, joy, peace, patience, kindness, goodness, faithfulness, gentleness, and self-control.

We can try to be joyful, kind, and good in our own power, but eventually, we'll run out of motivation if we're the source. Have you ever felt this way? You try hard to love that person in your life who just frustrates you so much . . . and eventually you run out of patience. I can relate!

It is only through the power of the Spirit that we are able to do what God asks of us. Earlier in Galatians 5, Paul explains what life by the Spirit looks like: serving one another humbly in love and loving our neighbor as ourselves (vv. 13–14). When we walk by the Spirit, we are an outpouring of God's love on the world. The Holy Spirit enables us to love others (Rom. 5:5). We can experience the fruit of the Spirit no matter our circumstances. We can be content in all situations (Phil. 4:11–13).

For many years, I thought the main purpose of the Holy Spirit was to empower me to serve God. That is one of his purposes, but he's so much more than that. In college, I learned how to walk with God and was struck by the invitation he gives his people to impact others, through sharing our faith. I knew I needed the Holy Spirit to do that, but what I didn't realize until years later was that I needed the Holy Spirit just to live the Christian life. I couldn't share about Jesus in my own power, but I also couldn't walk with God each day through my own power. When I realized this, I enjoyed the Christian life much more. I experienced more fruit of the Spirit and, unsurprisingly, I naturally wanted to talk about Jesus more because I was experiencing his goodness through the Spirit on a consistent basis.

I don't use the Holy Spirit to serve God or to get in his good graces. The Holy Spirit is not to be used for justification in our own effort. The Holy Spirit brings intimacy with God. He brings joy in the ups and downs of life. He gives us comfort and peace in the midst of hard things. He helps us live the Christian life, which is impossible to live without him.

The Holy Spirit also helps us know God and ourselves. He opens our eyes to who God is and how he's at work in our lives. He illuminates Scripture to help us understand the things of God (1 Cor. 2:12–14). The Spirit grows our intimacy with God as we pray, read Scripture, and commune with God.

***

"The Spirit of the Father and the Son would never be interested in merely empowering us to 'do good.' His desire (which is the desire of the Father and the Son) is to bring us to such a hearty enjoyment of God through Christ that we delight to know him, that we delight in all his ways, and that therefore we want to do as he wants and we hate the thought of ever grieving him."

—Michael Reeves, *Delighting in the Trinity*[1]

I am a worshipper.

Among the gods there is none like you, Lord; no deeds can compare with yours. All the nations you have made will come and worship before you, Lord; they will bring glory to your name. For you are great and do marvelous deeds; you alone are God.

—Psalm 86:8–10

Worship is an expression of adoration and reverence. We can worship in a variety of ways. While music is a common method of praising God, it's far from the only way to do so. We worship God with our thoughts, our words, and how we live our lives. We worship him when we use the gifts he's given us to serve others. We worship him when we give money cheerfully and generously. Often, we feel God's presence through music when we are at church. But God's presence is everywhere, all the time, and he can be worshiped through many means.

No matter the way we worship—with instruments, with liturgy, or with our actions—we are to worship God in spirit and in truth (John 4:24). For he is Spirit, and he is truth. To worship God only in truth can lead to pride in our theological views or to disengaged hearts. To worship God only in spirit can lead us down a path where only our emotional response is important. Both spirit and truth are essential.

The Psalms are full of lyrics written in response to God's character and his work in the world. They are honest and raw reflections on the state of the heart and circumstances of life. But they are also full of hope, proclaiming the goodness of God and the reality that he alone is worthy of our adoration.

Humans are conditioned to worship. It's ingrained in us. The question is, what will we worship? The choices are endless: ourselves (ego, pride, skills, abilities), our relationships (spouse, children, parents, friends), our financial state, our careers, or our dreams. If we are not careful, these things can all become idols, taking the place of God in our lives. It is tempting to worship and serve the things God created instead of the Creator himself (Rom. 1:25). We are transformed by whatever we choose to love. And we worship whatever we love.

Who (and what) we worship impacts how we live our lives, including how we work. In the book *The Practice of the Presence of God*, Brother Lawrence describes a deep connection with God. Throughout his days of menial tasks in a monastery, such as sweeping and doing the dishes, Brother Lawrence maintains a connection with God that is not dependent on the activity of his hands. He describes experiencing God's presence as a delight to his soul. The work we do flows out of our connection to God and is our act of worship. In the words of A.W. Tozer, "God wants worshippers first. Jesus did not redeem us to make us workers; He redeemed us to make us worshippers. And then, out of the blazing worship of our hearts, springs our work."[1]

Regular worship reminds us that our lives are not about us. Worship takes our eyes off our circumstances, worries, and day-to-day concerns and lifts them to God. Being connected with a local body of believers in a church helps to give us much-needed perspective.

When we come to worship with others, we collectively experience the Spirit of God moving in our midst. We agree on the truth of who God is. We are reminded that we are part of a larger body of Christ. Yes, in some seasons of life, it can be hard to make it a priority to attend worship services. Yes, the local church is a messy place, and sometimes, it causes very real hurt. But to persevere through the ups and downs in a safe environment with other like-minded people who are also trusting God grows us in a way that nothing else can. We grow in love and unity with our brothers and sisters in Christ.

We can worship God at any moment, through any method. We can worship privately or in a crowd of so many people that we can't count them all. We will face real temptations to worship things that we love that are not God. God is gracious with us, but he is also jealous. He wants our affection and devotion.

***

"Has it ever occurred to you that one hundred pianos all tuned to the same fork are automatically tuned to each other? They are of one accord by being tuned, not to each other, but to another standard to which each one must individually bow. So one hundred worshipers met together, each one looking away to Christ, are in heart nearer to each other than they could possibly be, were they to become 'unity' conscious and turn their eyes away from God to strive for closer fellowship."

—A.W. Tozer, *The Pursuit of God*[2]

I am a temple.

Don't you know that you yourselves are God's temple and
that God's Spirit dwells in your midst?

—1 Corinthians 3:16

In the Old Testament, God's Spirit dwelt in the tabernacle, a tent that the Israelites would move around as
they traveled. God gave Moses instructions for building
the tabernacle, taking multiple chapters in Exodus to explain the types of materials to use and how to build it
correctly. Chapter after chapter in 1 Chronicles, God
gives Solomon instructions for building the temple, a
more permanent place for God to be with his people.

While God's presence continues to dwell in brick-
and-mortar buildings, he also dwells within his people.
When we place our faith in Christ, the Holy Spirit enters
us, and we are empowered by him. The Spirit is always
there, aiding us in every part of the Christian life. While
we are always filled with the Holy Spirit, we yield control to him on a moment-by-moment basis, walking
step-by-step with him. The Spirit is always within us,
but we actively choose to walk in his power and not in
our own.

A temple is a sacred place. In the Jerusalem temple and the movable tabernacle, there was an innermost place, called the holy of holies. Only the priests who were chosen by God and had purified themselves could enter. The Israelites also needed to be purified before entering the temple courts. God is serious about holiness.

While we no longer follow the priestly laws from the Old Testament, we do need to consider how we create a space for God to reside in us. God is present everywhere but also inside of us: "Do you not know that your bodies are temples of the Holy Spirit, who is in you, whom you have received from God? You are not your own; you were bought at a price. Therefore honor God with your bodies" (1 Cor. 6:19–20).

Jesus paid the highest price by giving his life to pay for sin. This truth is not meant to pressure us to live up to a perfect standard of holiness and sinlessness that only Jesus could achieve. The recognition of this undeserved gift—the reality that we are a place where God dwells—moves us to gratitude. And in response, we care well for our bodies. We want to steward our bodies well to honor God.

God calls us to be living sacrifices, holy and pleasing to him. This is an act of worship to God (Rom. 12:1). Our bodies are not our own, so we surrender them to God. We care for them because they are a gift from God, even if they don't look like or work like we hope. We don't treat our bodies as worthless. We treat them with care and respect.

Collectively, we are all temples for God to dwell in. His presence is everywhere at all times, and he can reside in each of us at once. Ephesians 2:19–22 describes what it looks like when we are all together temples of God:

> Consequently, you are no longer foreigners and strangers, but fellow citizens with God's people and also members of his household, built on the foundation of the apostles and prophets, with Christ Jesus himself as the chief cornerstone. In him the whole building is joined together and rises to become a holy temple in the Lord. And in him you too are being built together to become a dwelling in which God lives by his Spirit.

The church is more than a building; the church is the family of God coming together. That reality helps me understand the above passage from Ephesians 2 in a new light: Jesus is the cornerstone upon which everything is built. God's people—members of his household—join together to be built into a place where God dwells among us, together. First Peter 2:4–5 calls Jesus and his followers living stones: "As you come to him, the living Stone—rejected by humans but chosen by God and precious to him—you also, like living stones, are being built into a spiritual house to be a holy priesthood, offering spiritual sacrifices acceptable to God through Jesus Christ." This holy priesthood is part of our identity, too:

> But you are a chosen people, a royal priesthood, a holy nation, God's special possession, that you may

declare the praises of him who called you out of darkness into his wonderful light. Once you were not a people, but now you are the people of God; once you had not received mercy, but now you have received mercy. (1 Pet. 2:9–10)

Because of this, believers in Jesus are part of the priesthood. We have access to God just as the priests did, but we don't make animal sacrifices. Instead, we go boldly to God's throne of grace, in confidence, and he hears us (Heb. 4:16). We come to God as we are, failures and flaws on full display, and he empathizes with our weaknesses (Heb. 4:15). We are invited to be living sacrifices, giving our bodies to God (Rom. 12:1). We do so out of love and obedience, not obligation.

***

"An altar is a place of interaction between the God of heaven and a man or woman on earth. It's the meeting place where a merger is forged between the heart of God and the heart of the worshiper. You can't have an altar without a sacrifice. Jesus is the ultimate sacrifice for us; he has already paid the price for us by giving his life. However, each of us can also offer our lives to God in love, adoration, and service toward him."

—Mark E Strong, *A Just Passion*[3]

I am a branch on the vine.

I am the true vine, and my Father is the gardener. He cuts off every branch in me that bears no fruit, while every branch that does bear fruit he prunes so that it will be even more fruitful. You are already clean because of the word I have spoken to you. Remain in me, as I also remain in you. No branch can bear fruit by itself; it must remain in the vine. Neither can you bear fruit unless you remain in me. I am the vine; you are the branches. If you remain in me and I in you, you will bear much fruit; apart from me you can do nothing. If you do not remain in me, you are like a branch that is thrown away and withers; such branches are picked up, thrown into the fire and burned. If you remain in me and my words remain in you, ask whatever you wish, and it will be done for you. This is to my Father's glory, that you bear much fruit, showing yourselves to be my disciples.

—John 15:1–8

John 15 is one of my favorite chapters of the Bible. It is part of the last set of messages Jesus gives to his disciples the last night he spends with them, before being arrested and ultimately going to the cross. In this chapter, Jesus uses the imagery of a vine to explain the way we are to live as believers—as branches of that vine.

God is the vine to which we are connected in this life; he sustains us as we remain in him. To abide in Christ means to remain connected to him all the time. When I sit and think about what this means, I realize how gracious God is that He would even *allow* us to abide in Him. He, a holy and just God who cannot tolerate sin, allows us to be in his presence because Jesus's death pays the debt we owe. He makes us right with God and allows us to experience his presence (Eph. 3:12).

He desires for us to come to him (Ps. 145:18) with all of our needs and wants (Heb. 4:16). He gives us access to himself (Eph. 2:18). He longs to be with us, and he desires we be with him (John 17:24). He longs for us to abide in him, that we might know him, and he might know us.

We can be tempted to look to other sources in place of Christ as the true vine. These are often good things that will help us grow and bear fruit, but they are not Jesus. Parents, siblings, pastors, friends, a spouse, favorite authors or theologians, and on and on. All of these relationships or influences in our lives can help us grow closer to God and experience him in our lives. But this passage is clear that Jesus is the vine that we are to remain connected to. He describes himself as the true vine—true meaning ultimate. He is most important. Most significant. Most trustworthy. These other sources that encourage and motivate us can be good, but they are not the ultimate source.

This includes us. One of the hardest things for me to realize as I live the Christian life is that I am not my own vine. I think I can just pull myself up by my bootstraps and try a little harder to do the things I should do. But I can't be both the branch and the vine. If I'm the branch, by default I'm not the vine. I am unable to sustain myself in life, and neither can you. We can't muster up the motivation we need to do hard things, like be patient with our kids, spouse, or roommate. We may think we can, and we may try to do it out of our own willpower, determination, or strength. But eventually, we fail.

This is good news! Life is much better connected to the vine, even if we were able to live without it. Jesus repeats himself over and over in John 15: We abide in Christ because he is the only lasting source of life. Apart from abiding in Christ, we can do nothing. If we do not remain in Christ, we will wither.

A vine doesn't exist simply to be a pretty element in nature. Its purpose is not to look good, but to feed nutrients to its branches, which grow fruit. The branch exists for a purpose, and the health of the branch is seen by the fruit it bears. As we remain connected to Christ, this fruit will flow out of our lives naturally. Bearing fruit means to grow in character—to become more like Christ and reflect the fruit of the Spirit (Gal. 5:22–23). The fruit that Jesus speaks of here is evidence of a relationship with him.

We, individually, are branches on the vine. But what does it mean that we, collectively, are branches on the vine? We grow alongside each other. We produce fruit together. Some branches produce more fruit, and that's okay. Growth is not a competition. We don't manufacture bearing more fruit to keep up with the other branches; we grow what we are given to grow. We get pruned, some of us more than others. Some pruning is public, some is private. But with this pruning, we may bear more fruit than we ever thought possible, all for the glory of God.

***

"And all the branch possesses belongs to the vine. The branch does not exist for itself, but to bear fruit that can proclaim the excellence of the vine: it has no reason of existence except to be of service to the vine. Glorious image of the calling of the believer, and the entireness of his consecration to the service of his Lord."

—Andrew Murray, *Abide in Christ*[4]

I am created by God.

For you created my inmost being; you knit me together in
my mother's womb. I praise you because I am fearfully and
wonderfully made; your works are wonderful, I know that
full well. My frame was not hidden from you when I was
made in the secret place, when I was woven together in the
depths of the earth. Your eyes saw my unformed body; all
the days ordained for me were written in your book before
one of them came to be.

—Psalm 139:13–16

All of humanity is created in the image of God, regardless of one's beliefs or background. Being created in the
image of God is a foundational part of who we are. God
created the heavens and the earth, and everything in
them (Col. 1:16). But he created humans to be unique
and distinct from the rest of creation. We were made in
God's image (Gen. 1:27), the only aspect of creation to
be made this way. This elevates the status of human beings above the rest of creation and gives each individual
person inherent dignity and worth. We were formed out
of dust (Gen. 2:7) and are now being transformed into
the likeness of Christ (Rom. 8:29). From nothing, we become something. God continually shapes us throughout
our lives, creating and recreating us all the time.

Because we are created, we create. God has given each of us passions and skills to create something from nothing, just as he did in creating us. Not only does he allow us to take part in creating, but he loves it when we do. He created us in his image, and so, like him, we also create.

Recently, a friend remarked she didn't see herself as creative. Upon questioning her, I discovered that she (like many of us) was interpreting "creative" to mean "artistic" (drawing, painting, decorating her home, etc.). I prodded her to dig deeper, assuring her that she was creative in some way, it just might not look like the traditional expressions we commonly think about.

Through our dialogue, she realized she enjoys creating fun environments where people enjoy each other's company. She likes creating order, a characteristic that mirrors God, who created an orderly world separated into sea and land, sky and earth, day and night. While some of us are artistic or crafty and produce beautiful, physical things, others are gifted at creating intangible things. For example, someone could create a warm and inviting home where people experience connection with others and where people feel like they can truly be themselves without fear of judgment. This is no small thing! God longs for us to create things that will reflect his beauty in this world and will serve others.

If you struggle to think of yourself as creative, ask yourself: *What do I love? How do I like to use my imagination? What do I enjoy doing so much that while doing it, I lose track of time?* These are indicators of your creativity. God has given you a unique personality, imagination, and desires. You are able to combine those in a way that offers something to the world that no one else can. Like making a loaf of bread from a few simple ingredients, we can take simple things in front of us and make a masterpiece—just as God did in creating us from dust. Just like God did in creating a masterpiece of us (Eph. 2:10).

In the Old Testament, we read about the people of God using their resources and skills to help build and design the tabernacle—the place where God's manifest presence would reside. The Israelites brought their goods to the Lord as an offering, using what they had to construct the tent of meeting. They offered up precious metals, fine linens and yarn, animal hair and leather, acacia wood, olive oil and spices, stones and gems. Workers were needed to cut and set stones, carpenters were needed to construct the frame and furniture, and designers were needed to engage in various artistic crafts like engraving, embroidering, and weaving (Exod. 35). What an incredible picture of what happens when the body of believers brings the skills and gifts they have to offer up to the Lord.

We are created for good works and can use our creativity to honor God and serve others. Even if we don't have creative gifts that are considered traditional or popular, every one of us is creative in some way. God has given all of us an imagination and a unique set of skills. Do what comes naturally to you—writing, sewing, woodworking, repairing, programming, baking, styling hair, designing, organizing, photography, and so much more.

Your gifts might not be the traditional artistic kind, but don't fall into the comparison trap; use what God gave you to love and serve others, and joy will follow because God delights when his people honor the way they are created.

***

"Human creativity, then, images God's creativity when it emerges from a lively, loving community of persons and, perhaps more important, when it participates in unlocking the full potential of what has gone before and creating possibilities for what will come later."

—Andy Crouch, *Culture Making: Recovering Our Creative Calling*[5]

5

I am impacting others.

God invites us to make a difference in the world. He not only invites us, he's created us with that desire. We are wired to make a difference, to make our community a better place, and to have a positive impact on others. As believers, we work for the good of others (Gal. 6:9). We love one another, as Christ has loved us (John 13:34). There are as many ways to make an impact as there are people in the world. And everyone plays a part in making a difference. We need everyone in the body of Christ.

We learn and grow and change while we follow Christ. But if we aren't reaching others, we're missing out on part of how God is at work in and through us. If we have experienced the life-changing transformation of the gospel that God can bring, why would we keep that to ourselves?

Throughout the gospels, we see Jesus inviting others to come and follow him. In John 10, Jesus describes himself as the Good Shepherd, and his followers, his sheep. In verse 16, he describes his people as one flock, under one shepherd. He wants all of his people to be together under his authority and care. He pursues his sheep, but we can pursue them too.

Making an impact has always been on my mind. Even as a little kid, I wanted to do something significant with my life. I didn't know what it was, but I knew I didn't like the status quo. I thought maybe I'd get a good-paying job and make a ton of money and then give it all away when I died. And believe me, that is one legitimate way to impact others.

But when I started to follow Jesus, my goals started to change. I saw the value in personal relationships with others—that one conversation or helpful act could make a difference in the life of someone else. Rather than wait until I died to hope I could make some kind of impact, I realized that I could start right away, as a broke college student who was learning who she was in Christ and was seeing it change her life. I started to see that the little things in life mattered.

I also started to see that being a part of a group of people who wanted to impact others mattered. I saw the influence that my community of friends could have as a group. Together, the body of Christ plays a part in how God works in the world. Together, we are making a difference. When we pool our time, our talents, our desires, and other resources, our ability to influence grows. We're supported by each other when our motivation wanes. We are reminded that our lives are not just about ourselves.

Acts 2 is a classic passage about the community of believers impacting others:

> They devoted themselves to the apostles' teaching and to fellowship, to the breaking of bread and to prayer. Everyone was filled with awe at the many wonders and signs performed by the apostles. All the believers were together and had everything in common. They sold property and possessions to give to anyone who had need. Every day they continued to meet in the temple courts. They broke bread in their homes and ate together with glad and sincere hearts, praising God and enjoying the favor of all the people. And the Lord added to their number daily those who were being saved. (Acts 2:42–47)

The early church followers lived life in community. They reallocated resources to those who had need. They worshipped and prayed together. They ate together, giving thanks and enjoying one another. And people's lives were impacted in a positive way, as day by day, more people came to know Jesus.

Throughout Scripture, God encourages and instructs his people to seek justice (Isa. 1:17; Micah 6:8). There are hundreds of verses about caring for the poor, the widows, the orphans, and the oppressed. Justice done in the name of God is an act of love and reconciliation. We can make a difference in the world by righting wrongs, restoring power imbalances, and working for the good of others.

Justice is at the very heart of God (Ps. 9:7–8; Isa. 61:8). As we are made in his image, we reflect his heart to the world. The life you live is preaching a message. What is it saying? When given the chance, what are you preaching with your words?

In this section, we focus on impacting others: We are witnesses, we are aromas, we are gifted, we are ambassadors for Christ, and we are vessels.

I am a witness.

Come and listen, all you who fear God,
and I will tell you what he did for me.

—Psalm 66:16 NLT

John the Baptist prepared the way for Jesus, calling for repentance and proclaiming forgiveness of sins. John was a witness who could testify to the light of Jesus. John himself was not the light; he came only as a witness to the light (John 1:8).

When confronted by Jewish priests and Levites who asked him who he was, John was quick to confess that he was not the Messiah. He saw and testified that Jesus was the chosen one. John knew who he was (a messenger, a witness), and who he was not (the Messiah).

We are like John, messengers and witnesses about who Jesus is to those around us. When I think of being a witness, I think of it as a verb. I witness to others about my faith in Jesus. But "witness" is also a noun. In a courtroom, a witness tells everyone what they have seen and experienced. Their accurate testimony helps prove what happened.

You have seen and experienced Jesus at work in your life; therefore, you are a witness. This is where the verb comes from. We are a witness, and we've witnessed God at work. How has he been at work? How has he changed your heart? How has he corrected you, encouraged you, or led you to do something you never thought you could do?

Jesus calls John a burning lamp, showing others the way to Jesus. But Jesus was an even greater witness than John; his teachings and miracles proved that Jesus was sent to earth by God to reconcile us to him (John 5:33, 35).

Throughout Scripture, regular people see Jesus at work right in front of them. After they experience him, they tell others what he has done for them. The Samaritan woman at the well meets Jesus as he crosses cultural lines to connect with her. She can't help but tell those in her home, "Come, see a man who told me everything I ever did. Could this be the Messiah?" (John 4:29). They went to Jesus to see for themselves. And many other Samaritans believed in him because of the woman's testimony (John 4:39). They asked Jesus to stay with them, and he stayed two more days. As a result, many more people put their faith in Jesus. "They said to the woman, 'We no longer believe just because of what you said; now we have heard for ourselves, and we know that this man really is the Savior of the world'" (John 4:42).

What if the woman had kept this good news to herself? What if she had been too embarrassed by her story, uncertain of how others might perceive her? She throws off any concern for what people might think, and as a result, people are saved.

Collectively, we are witnesses. Together with the family of believers, we can remind each other of how we've witnessed God at work in our lives, which gives us hope when we doubt his presence or promises. Hebrews 11 gives a laundry list of people who lived by faith and trusted God: Abel, Enoch, Noah, Abraham, Sarah, Isaac, Jacob, Joseph, Moses, Rahab, Gideon, and more. Hebrews 12 calls them a "great cloud of witnesses," and we are part of that group as well.

Together, we witness to the world about the great things Jesus has done. There were more than five hundred witnesses to Jesus's resurrection (1 Cor. 15:6). Seeing a man come back from the dead was likely one of the most incredible things these witnesses had ever experienced. I imagine that they could not keep these encounters to themselves, and their experience of Jesus led to the spreading of the gospel in the early church. After the resurrection, Jesus ascended to heaven and explained what was next for his church: "You will receive power when the Holy Spirit comes upon you. And you will be my witnesses, telling people about me everywhere—in Jerusalem, throughout Judea, in Samaria, and to the ends of the earth" (Acts 1:8 NLT). Witnessing to others about Jesus always comes after an experience of him in our lives.

We are all witnesses to what Jesus has done for us as individuals, but also to what he has done collectively in the church. Regularly sharing with one another what God is doing in our own lives encourages and builds each other up. We need to remind each other of the good work God has done and of his good character. We don't only witness to those who do not believe, but also to those who believe. We do not share to brag or boast, but because the love of Christ motivates us to do so (2 Cor. 5:14).

***

"The best witness we have as the church is not our good music, nor the programs that meet felt needs, nor the quality of the edifice that people worship in. The best witness we have is our transformed lives."

—Rich Villodas, *The Deeply Formed Life*[1]

I am an aroma.

Follow God's example, therefore, as dearly loved children and walk in the way of love, just as Christ loved us and gave himself up for us as a fragrant offering and sacrifice to God.

—Ephesians 5:1–2

You may know the Bible story of the great flood that wiped out all of humanity except for Noah and his family. God asks Noah to build an ark, and he does, gathering two of every animal to join him. The rain comes, the earth floods, and, well, you know. Noah and his family waited for the rain to stop and then for the earth to dry. They spent more than a *year* on the ark. When they emerged, the first thing Noah did was build an altar to sacrifice burnt offerings to God. "And the LORD was pleased with the aroma of the sacrifice" (Gen. 8:21 NLT).

Forty times in the Old Testament, an aroma is mentioned in the context of an offering made to the Lord. And every time it's mentioned, the word "pleasing" is included. The sacrifices made to God to atone for (meaning to make up for) sin were pleasing to him.

This Old Testament sacrificial system was set up so people could atone for their brokenness and be made right with God. There were all kinds of sacrifices and offerings to be made for different reasons and at different times of the year. But the system wasn't perfect. Could the blood of an animal really atone for the sins of humanity?

Jesus changed everything. We no longer live according to the Old Testament system of animal sacrifices and offerings. Jesus lived the perfect life we couldn't, and died a cruel death on a cross, as a sacrifice for us. We now live as a pleasing aroma to God, accepted by him through Jesus Christ:

> Our lives are a Christ-like fragrance rising up to God. But this fragrance is perceived differently by those who are being saved and by those who are perishing. To those who are perishing, we are a dreadful smell of death and doom. But to those who are being saved, we are a life-giving perfume. And who is adequate for such a task as this? (2 Cor. 2:15–16 NLT)

Aroma is powerful: fresh-cut grass, baking bread, a pile of garbage on a hot day. Individually, aroma is powerful, but in community, the power of an aroma is multiplied. Imagine walking into your kitchen and taking a fresh-baked loaf of bread out of the oven. Now imagine walking down a street with a dozen bakeries, all making fresh bread. The aroma is inescapable. It permeates everything. It's like coming inside after a bonfire and realizing all your clothes smell like smoke. Or returning home from a coffee shop to realize you smell like roasted coffee beans.

We are a fragrance that is unavoidable to the world. As we, as a community, live as sacrifices pleasing to God, people cannot help but take notice. To those who do not follow Christ, our lives may not make much sense. This aroma that is pleasing to God may not smell good to those who don't understand why we live the way we do. But to those searching for God, our aroma attracts. It causes people to consider why we are different. There is significance in this collective aroma. Like one light bulb illuminates a street corner, a row of lights up and down the block changes the whole street.

As a newer believer, the aroma I noticed was the joy in my friends' lives. Their lives weren't perfect; they had troubles just like everyone else, but they lived with a certainty in the sovereignty of God. They knew he loved and cared for them. Anything they might be worried about was in his hands. They were so secure in and certain of his love for them that they didn't need the acceptance and approval of others, which was what I was mostly concerned with.

Jesus offered up his life as a fragrant offering and sacrifice to God. We are to follow this example and walk in the way of love (Eph. 5:2). We are instructed to be living sacrifices to God (Rom. 12:1), laying our lives before him in surrender as we walk with him each day.

***

"The sweetest fragrance, the most beautiful aroma that God has ever detected emanating from this planet, was the aroma of the perfect sacrifice of Jesus that was offered once and for all on the cross."

—R.C. Sproul, *The Purpose of God*[2]

I am gifted.

Each of you should use whatever gift you have received to serve others, as faithful stewards of God's grace in its various forms. If anyone speaks, they should do so as one who speaks the very words of God. If anyone serves, they should do so with the strength God provides, so that in all things God may be praised through Jesus Christ. To him be the glory and the power for ever and ever. Amen.

—1 Peter 4:10–11

We are gifted by God for the purposes and good works he has planned for us (Eph. 2:10). He has given his people specific spiritual gifts that we can use to serve his church and the world. A spiritual gift is an ability from the Holy Spirit used to serve others. There are several lists of spiritual gifts in Scripture:

> To one there is given through the Spirit a message of wisdom, to another a message of knowledge by means of the same Spirit, to another faith by the same Spirit, to another gifts of healing by that one Spirit, to another miraculous powers, to another prophecy, to another distinguishing between spirits, to another speaking in different kinds of tongues, and to still another

the interpretation of tongues. All these are the work of one and the same Spirit, and he distributes them to each one, just as he determines. (1 Cor. 12:8–11)

We have different gifts, according to the grace given to each of us. If your gift is prophesying, then prophesy in accordance with your faith; if it is serving, then serve; if it is teaching, then teach; if it is to encourage, then give encouragement; if it is giving, then give generously; if it is to lead, do it diligently; if it is to show mercy, do it cheerfully. (Rom. 12:6–8)

These are not exhaustive lists but give a solid picture of what spiritual gifts God has given to his people. Everyone has at least one spiritual gift. Some may have a few. God has created you uniquely and invites you to use your giftings to impact the church and the world.

Before he writes about spiritual gifts in Romans 12:6–8, Paul describes the context in which we are to use our gifts. We are to offer ourselves up as living sacrifices as an act of worship (Rom. 12:1). We are to use our giftings not to build ourselves up, but to serve those around us with humility (Rom. 12:3). God gives us spiritual gifts to varying degrees and for various functions, and by living these out we make up our part of the larger body of Christ (Rom. 12:3–5).

In a similar way, 1 Corinthians 12 lists spiritual gifts in the context of unity and servanthood. It is the same Spirit who gives all gifts (1 Cor. 12:4) and different kinds of service, but the same God being honored (1 Cor. 12:5). There is no room for competition in the living out of spiritual gifts. We must be unified, serving the entire body of Christ and our world as a whole. There are different kinds of gifts, but in all of them and in everyone it is the same God at work (1 Cor. 12:6). These gifts are given for the common good (1 Cor. 12:7)—not so that we will take pride in ourselves but so that we give all glory to God.

We are not to compare ourselves with others and the gifts they have, but we are to come together with others, as parts of one body, in unity and diversity (1 Cor. 12:12–14). No part of the body is less honorable or weaker based on the gifts they have (1 Cor. 12:22–23). No one person has all of the spiritual gifts, which shows our need for others in the body of Christ (1 Cor. 12:29–30). We all play a vital role.

Along with this, not all people with the same gifts receive them to the same degree (Rom. 12:6). We are given different measures of grace. We can hone our gifts over time to grow stronger in them. Again, we are not to compare ourselves with others and the way they use their gifts. We are each uniquely gifted and called to use those gifts in the way God desires. This calling may look different for you than for someone else with a similar gift.

If you are not sure what your gifts are, there are several ways to find out. Pray and ask God to reveal to you what your gifts are as you read through the above passages. Ask a few trusted friends or a mentor what they think your giftings might be. You can take a spiritual gifts assessment (your pastor or church staff may have recommendations). Perhaps best of all, start serving in your church and see where you thrive.

Finally, a gentle reminder: We do not earn God's grace in our lives by serving him. We do not earn his favor or love by using our gifts. But by discovering and using them, we are given a chance to love and serve others and bring glory to God. We get the privilege of being used by him to impact his world for good.

***

"Without each person knowing and using their spiritual gifts, the body of Christ is incomplete and is hindered from reaching its full potential."

—Renee Swope, *A Confident Heart*[3]

I am an ambassador for Christ.

And all of this is a gift from God, who brought us back to himself through Christ. And God has given us this task of reconciling people to him. For God was in Christ, reconciling the world to himself, no longer counting people's sins against them. And he gave us this wonderful message of reconciliation. So we are Christ's ambassadors; God is making his appeal through us. We speak for Christ when we plead, "Come back to God!" For God made Christ, who never sinned, to be the offering for our sin, so that we could be made right with God through Christ.

—2 Corinthians 5:18–21 NLT

A foreign ambassador has the privilege to represent their country of citizenship. They are appointed, confirmed, and accredited to serve in this way, and with this title comes duties and responsibilities. They do not lobby for themselves and their own agenda, but that of the entity they represent.

We are ambassadors for Christ, here to represent him to the world. We are citizens of heaven (Phil. 3:20) and members of the kingdom of God (Col. 1:13). He has authorized us to have this great honor and duty of being an ambassador.

Paul unpacks this idea in 2 Corinthians 5:18–21. Before this section, Paul writes about the love of Christ. It is through this lens of love that we view our role as ambassadors. "[Christ] died for everyone so that those who receive his new life will no longer live for themselves. Instead, they will live for Christ, who died and was raised for them" (2 Cor. 5:15). We are dead to our old life, which was all about ourselves. In this old life, we were only concerned about getting ahead, competing with others, and taking whatever we wanted just because we could. This new life means putting off the old self and taking up the new self, with a new identity as a representative of Christ, not ourselves.

You are an ambassador, meant to usher in reconciliation so that others may be made right with God through Christ. We do not bring our own agenda to accomplish. We do not represent Christ because we're right and we want to lord it over others. We don't do it to fill seats in our churches or to prove we're good Christians. We don't do it to gain political power or win elections. We represent Christ to a broken and hopeless world because the love of Christ compels us (2 Cor. 5:14). We represent Christ to the world because he loves us, and now we love others. He has transformed us from the inside out, and we want others to experience that transformation too.

Ambassadors fight for reconciliation, which includes fighting for unity and peace. When the body of Christ is fighting with itself, why would we expect anyone to want to follow Jesus? If we can't have unity within the family of God, why would anyone want to join it? Ambassadors work toward peace and unity.

In his Sermon on the Mount, Jesus describes characteristics that he wants his followers to emulate. Among them is to be peacemakers, "for they will be called children of God" (Matt. 5:9). It is pivotal to our identity as children of God that we be peacemakers.

Peacemaking is not the same as peacekeeping. We do not shy away from speaking truth in love. We uphold our convictions and beliefs. But we do so respectfully and honorably. We recognize when we are wrong. We don't fight over inconsequential opinions or issues. We seek unity and reconciliation with others and with God. He desires reconciliation with his people, and we can offer that to a world that is broken and without hope. A world full of people who are made in the image of God, who have dignity and worth.

How does it feel that God would trust you with being an ambassador, giving you the ministry of reconciliation? Heavy? Overwhelming? Exciting? God is not expecting perfection, and he doesn't give you this title to put pressure on you. Being an ambassador is an invitation to represent him. He equips those he calls to serve and will be with you every step of the way.

***

"A corporate witness to the reality of reconciliation is a perfect demonstration of the gospel. Our unity in the midst of our diversity is one of the most powerful ways we reveal the reality of what Jesus accomplished on the cross."

—Brenda Salter McNeil, *A Just Passion*[4]

I am a vessel.

Therefore, if anyone cleanses himself from what is dishonorable, he will be a vessel for honorable use, set apart as holy, useful to the master of the house, ready for every good work.

—2 Timothy 2:21 ESV

The whole point of the Christian life is to become more like Jesus. This is called sanctification. This happens not in a moment but over the course of a lifetime. Throughout this process, we become more aware of our brokenness and bring it to God, who is kind and patient with us. He cleanses us from our sin and sets us apart for honorable use.

God created us as vessels for him to dwell within us. We are a place for God to live and a place for him to enjoy being at home in us. This happens as we are sanctified. As we grow closer to Christ, the old things we used to love don't satisfy us, and the things of God do. We make more room for him, and he makes more of his home in us.

We are vessels, not only for God to dwell in, but for God to flow through. We can show others who God is by being a vessel of his love, joy, peace, forbearance, kindness, goodness, faithfulness, gentleness, and self-control (Gal. 5:22–23). This is the fruit of the Holy Spirit at work in our lives. We don't manufacture these good things, trying to live them out through our own will-power. We rely on his Spirit living in us to help us become more like him and embody these characteristics to the world around us.

God can take an ordinary vessel like us and use it for good and for his glory. The first miracle of Jesus recorded in the Bible occurs at a wedding (John 2:1–12). Mary, the mother of Jesus, alerts him that the wine has run out. This is not a good situation for the bride and groom; it's a dishonor. Mary is hoping that Jesus can help them save face.

Jesus instructs the servants to take six stone water jars and fill them with water. The jars were used for ceremonial washing by the Jews, holding something like twenty gallons each. Once the jars are full, Jesus tells them to draw some water out and take it to the wedding master. He tries some and proclaims it to be the best wine of the night.

"What Jesus did here in Cana of Galilee was the first of the signs through which he revealed his glory; and his disciples believed in him" (John 2:11). God used those plain old vessels at the wedding to reveal his glory, and it resulted in people believing in him. God can do the same with us, taking ordinary vessels and using them for his good purposes.

In 2 Timothy 2:21, we read about four aspects of being a vessel. A vessel is:

~ for honorable use (pure and honest, with no hidden pretense).
~ set apart as holy (special and sacred, for a specific purpose).
~ useful to the master of the house (working on behalf of God, not us).
~ ready for every good work (at the ready, willing to say yes to God when he asks us to step out in faith).

Together, we are vessels. God dwells in each of us at the same time. We experience him in individual ways, and he has specific purposes for each of us. He creates each vessel differently, some out of gold, silver, wood, or clay. All are valuable to God because he loves each of us and created us.

We are vessels who let God live through us to be a light to those around us. The community of God is a vessel through which God ministers to the world. The world sees the way that followers of Jesus interact with each other and with those outside of the church. How we interact with others matters.

It's a lot of pressure, to be honest. We're not perfect. We make mistakes. We are broken people being redeemed and transformed by God. When we have fighting and disagreements within the body of Christ, it's hard to be a vessel. It's hard to be taken seriously by those outside of the church.

In John 17, Jesus talks about unity within the body of Christ. He prays for all believers to be in him, "so that the world may believe that you have sent me. I have given them the glory that you gave me, that they may be one as we are one—I in them and you in me—so that they may be brought to complete unity. Then the world will know that you sent me and have loved them even as you have loved me" (John 17:21–23).

We, the church, are to be one with each other, just as Jesus is one with God and the Holy Spirit. This is our witness to the world.

***

"The highest glory of the creature is in being a vessel, to receive and enjoy and show forth the glory of God. It can do this only as it is willing to be nothing in itself, that God may be everything."

—Andrew Murray, *Humility: The Journey Toward Holiness*[5]

Conclusion: I am beloved.

Who are you? How would you have answered that question before reading this book? How would you answer now?

Throughout the different stages of my life, I had different answers to the question: *Who am I?* I thought I needed to work to create my identity as the perfect Christian who had it all together. But as I pursued that, I felt like I could never live up to that standard. It turned out that I had created a persona in my mind of what I thought the perfect Christian should be.

All that I need to do is be the person God created me to be. I don't need to create that person myself; it's simply a discovery.

There are more aspects to our identity in Christ than I have listed in this book. But these have been some of the most significant to me as I've read Scripture and contemplated who I am in Christ. You may make other discoveries about your identity that are meaningful to you (I hope you do!).

My identity as the beloved is of greatest significance to me. But I don't hold a monopoly on that term; you are the beloved too. "Long ago the LORD said to Israel: 'I have loved you, my people, with an everlasting love. With unfailing love I have drawn you to myself'" (Jer. 31:3 NLT).

Throughout Scripture, the Israelites continue to make promises to God to follow his laws, and they continually let him down. And yet, God continues to pursue them. This doesn't mean they don't experience consequences from their disobedience, but God does not give up on them.

The Israelites give God every reason to quit loving them. As do we. But God's love for us is steady, unconditional, and relentless. It is everlasting, meaning it has no end, and it has no beginning. We are unworthy of God's love, and yet his love is high and wide and deep (Eph. 3:18).

God uses the term beloved to describe his son Jesus when he is baptized. In Matthew 3:17, God calls Jesus his beloved son, in whom he is pleased. Jesus hasn't even done anything yet. His ministry has not yet begun, but he knows who he is in the eyes of God.

This is how God looks at us, as well. We may question why, we may feel we haven't earned that love. And we haven't. But God desires to give it freely. All we need to do is acknowledge that we're never going to be able to earn it, and that Jesus is the reason we can claim this love we do not deserve.

We look to God to define us because he created us, knows us, and loves us unconditionally. Love comes from God because God *is* love. It is my hope and prayer that as a result of learning more about your identity in Christ, you will see yourself as he does: the beloved. It's my hope and prayer that as this reality sinks down deep into your heart and mind, it will change the way you live. You will experience more peace, knowing that you don't need to earn approval from God or others. You're already accepted in his eyes. You will experience more joy because you know that God cares deeply for you throughout the ups and downs of life. You will experience a deep sense of purpose, because you know that God has created you uniquely to impact those around you.

We are all the beloved of God. Being his beloved means you have all the love of God. He's infinite, so he can love each person with all of his love, and it never runs out. God never gets tired of loving you.

***

"An infinite God can give all of Himself to each of His children. He does not distribute Himself that each may have a part, but to each one He gives all of Himself as fully as if there were no others."

—A.W. Tozer, *The Pursuit of God*[6]

Acknowledgements

As you cannot live the Christian life in isolation, neither can you write a book. Thank you to those who have heard me talk at length about the concept of our collective identity in Christ!

Thank you to my very early beta readers: MJ, Jake, Julie F, Bethany A, Joi, Melissa M, Judy, Meghan, Allison, Ariahna, and Bethany B! This book took a turn from the early version, but your encouragement kept me going. Thanks to Judy and Abby for helping me get unstuck along the way, and to Rachel and Katelyn for being late-stage beta readers.

Thank you to my editor, Jana S, and cover designer, Karen C, who took this book to the next level in terms of professionalism. You both have mad skills!

Miracle City Church, Minneapolis: I am so thankful for you! I love how often we are encouraged to live out of our identity in Christ and to be the church, for each other, and for our community.

Thank you to my family, especially my mom, for instilling in me a love of reading at a young age. I don't know how many trips to the library we took when I was a kid, but I'm grateful you encouraged me.

And to MJ, Bethany, and Erika, who I'm sure got so, so sick of me talking about this book, hearing about my research, answering my requests for feedback . . . thank you. Remember that time I made you do that
activity at that pizza place in Rochester with the little slips of paper to help me organize the chapters???
Hahaha! It paid off. I'm so, so grateful for you guys.

About the Author

Amy Wellner has served in vocational ministry with Cru, a high school and college ministry, since 2009. She is a proud Minnesotan (her accent gives her away every time) and has lived in the Minneapolis area for fifteen years. She enjoys authentic conversations over a cup of coffee, as well as writing about identity and transformation. And yes, she really does love spreadsheets. She is also the author of *30 Days of Mark: Who Christ Is and How He Lived*.

Read more of her writing at: amywellner.com

Follow her on Instagram: @awellner

Notes

Section One

[1] Gospel in Life, "Basis of Prayer: 'Our Father' – Timothy Keller [Sermon]," August 10, 2015, https://www.youtube.com/watch?v=vqxXABgRhVo.
[2] Hosanna Wong, *You Are More Than You've Been Told* (Thomas Nelson, 2023), 8.
[3] Henri J.M. Nouwen, *Making All Things New: An Invitation to the Spiritual Life* (Harper San Francisco, 1981), 82–83.
[4] Brennan Manning, *The Furious Longing of God* (David C Cook, 2009), 24.
[5] Manning, *The Furious Longing of God*, 25.
[6] Elizabeth Garn, *Freedom to Flourish: The Rest God Offers in the Purpose He Gives You* (P & R Publishing, 2021), 28.
[7] Henri J.M. Nouwen, *Life of the Beloved: Spiritual Living in a Secular World* (Crossroad, 2002).

Section Two

[1] C.S. Lewis, *Mere Christianity* (HarperCollins, 1952), 136–137.
[2] Henri J.M. Nouwen, *You are the Beloved: 365 Daily Readings and Meditations for Spiritual Living* (The Henri Nouwen Legacy Trust, 2017), 99.
[3] Timothy Keller, *Center Church: Doing Balanced, Gospel-Centered Ministry in Your City* (Grand Rapids, MI: Zondervan, 2012), 172.
[4] "C. H. Spurgeon: Spurgeon's Sermons Volume 50: 1904," Christian Classics Ethereal Library, accessed Aug 14, 2025, https://ccel.org/ccel/spurgeon/sermons50/sermons50.xxii.html.
[5] Song lyrics by Trent Palmberg, "Inheritance," Miracle City Church, 2024.
[6] Dane C. Ortlund, *Gentle and Lowly* (Crossway, 2020), 175.

[7] Heather Holleman, *Seated with Christ: Living Freely in a Culture of Comparison* (Moody Publishers, 2015), 100.

Section Three

[1] Henry Cloud and John Townsend, *How People Grow: What the Bible Reveals about Personal Growth* (Zondervan, 2004), 22.
[2] "aphiemi," Blue Letter Bible, accessed April 27, 2025, https://www.blueletterbible.org/lexicon/g863/kjv/tr/0-1/.
[3] Timothy Keller, *Center Church: Doing Balanced, Gospel-Centered Ministry in Your City* (Grand Rapids, MI: Zondervan, 2012), 48.
[4] C.S. Lewis, *The Weight of Glory* (New York: HarperOne, 2001), 180.
[5] Dane C. Ortlund, *Deeper: Real Change for Real Sinners* (Wheaton, IL: Crossway, 2021), 118.
[6] Rachel Held Evans, *Faith Unraveled: How a Girl Who Knew All the Answers Learned to Ask Questions* (Grand Rapids, MI: Zondervan, 2014), 175.
[7] Corrie Ten Boom, *Each New Day* (Old Tappan, NJ: Fleming H. Revell Company, 1977).
[8] Rich Villodas, *Good and Beautiful and Kind: Becoming Whole in a Fractured World* (Colorado Springs, CO: WaterBrook, 2022), 72.

Section Four

[1] Michael Reeves, *Delighting in the Trinity* (Downers Grove, IL: InterVarsity Press, 2012), 101–102.
[2] A.W. Tozer, *The Pursuit of God* (Harrisburg, PA: Christian Publications, 1948), 90.
[3] Mark E. Strong, *A Just Passion* (Downers Grove, IL: InterVarsity Press, 2008), Kindle Edition, 39.
[4] Andrew Murray, *Abide in Christ: Thoughts on the Blessed Life of Fellowship with the Son of God* (New York: Anson D.F. Randolph & Co., 1864), 36.
[5] Andy Crouch, *Culture Making: Recovering Our Creative Calling*, Expanded ed. (Downers Grove, IL: InterVarsity Press, 2023), 105.

Section Five

[1] Rich Villodas, *The Deeply Formed Life: Five Transformative Values to Root Us in the Way of Jesus* (Colorado Springs, CO: WaterBrook, 2020), 217.

[2] R.C. Sproul, *The Purpose of God: Ephesians* (Christian Focus, 2011), 121.

[3] Renee Swope, *A Confident Heart: How to Stop Doubting Yourself and Live in the Security of God's Promises* (Revell, a division of Baker Publishing Group, 2011), 146.

[4] Brenda Salter McNeil, *A Just Passion* (Downers Grove, IL: InterVarsity Press, 2008), Kindle edition.

[5] Andrew Murray, *Humility: The Journey Toward Holiness* (Minneapolis: Bethany House Publishers, 2001), 99.

[6] A.W. Tozer, *The Pursuit of God* (Harrisburg, PA: Christian Publications, 1948), 46.